MW01245212

PANIC ATTACKS!

The Ultimate Practical MEDITATION GUIDE To Stop Worrying and Eliminate Negative Thinking

Anxiety and Panic Attacks:
How to overcome them and
Take back your life

By Steve Convey

Mira Star Publisher

Mira Star Publisher web site: www.mirastarpublisher.com

Important

The book is not intended to provide medical advice or to take the place of any treatment of your personal physician. Readers are advised to consult their own doctors or other qualified health professional regarding the treatment of medical conditions. The author shall not be held liable or responsible for any misunderstanding or misuse of the information contained in this book. The information is not indeed to diagnose, treat or cure any disease.

It's important to remember that the author of this book is not a doctor/therapist/medical professional. Only opinions based upon his own personal experiences or research are cited. The author does not offer medical advice or prescribe any treatments. For any health or medical issues – you should be talking to your doctor first.

DON'T ASSUME I'M WEAK

BECAUSE I HAVE PANIC ATTACKS.

YOU'LL NEVER KNOW

THE AMOUNT OF STRENGTH IT TAKES

TO FACE THE WORLD EVERY DAY.

- Quote -

TABLE OF CONTENTS

PANIC ATTACKS!

PREFACE

A panic attack is an extreme wave of anxiety marked by its unpredictability and weakening, immobilizing severity. Panic attacks are treatable, irrespective of the trigger. Panic attack signs and symptoms grow abruptly and typically reach their height within 10 minutes. Hyperventilation, heart pounding, chest pain, shaking, sweating, and dizziness can be signs of a panic attack, fear of losing control, going insane, or dying. While the precise causes of panic attacks and panic disorder are unknown, there is a propensity to experience panic attacks in families. A correlation with major life changes and extreme stress also appears to be present. Psychotherapy and medicine are used in care for panic attacks and panic disorders.

PANIC ATTACKS!

INTRODUCTION

An acute fear marked by the unexpectedness and immobilizing severity is a panic attack. Sometimes without warning, most often without a specific cause, hits can even occur when the person is comfortable or even asleep. There are common panic attacks. A panic disorder may be a one-time incident, but many individuals typically experience recurring episodes in a longer lifetime. The majority of people who ever had a PA had recurrent PAs (66.5, i.e., 0.5 percent). Most people recover without medication, and only a handful of them develop panic disorders from panic attacks. The lifetime prevalence of PAs is 13.2%(s.e. 0.1%). Recurrent panic attacks are often caused by a particular situation in which the person felt threatened before. As part of a different condition, such as panic disorder, social phobia, or depression, a panic attack can also occur. Panic attacks may be categorized into the following according to the relationship between the occurrence of the attack and the absence of involvement of situational triggers:

The most common form of attack in the PD is sudden (untested) panic attacks in which the occurrence of a panic attack is not linked to a circumstance cause (occurs unexpectedly as a lightning strike).

Situation-induced (triggered) panic attacks that occur almost always immediately after exposure or the expectation of a trigger situation (e.g., an immediate panic attack is often triggered by seeing a snake or dog).

Situationally predisposed panic attacks, which are strongly predicted to occur when exposed to the trigger scenario, but are not inseparably related to the trigger, and should not occur immediately after exposure (e.g., during the ride, panic attacks more likely to occur, but often people may drive and have no panic attacks, or they occur half an hour after the ride).

Other types of attacks include minimal symptoms and night attacks that occur in a special emotional sense.

Situational-induced attacks are more characteristic of social and specific phobias. In panic disorder, situationally predisposed panic attacks are especially prevalent but may also occur in real and social phobias. With or without agoraphobia, the onset of unexpected panic attacks is important for diagnosing panic disorder. The incidence of panic attacks and their intensity differ widely. For example, some people have intermediate-frequency attacks (e.g., once a week) that occur regularly for months. Others record regular short-term attacks (day, week) separated over a long period (weeks or months) without seizures or rare attacks (two per month) over a long period. Attacks with minimal symptoms are very common in panic disorders (e.g., similar to complete panic attacks, but with less associated symptoms).

A panic attack is intense anxiety characterized by unforeseenness and immobilizing intensity. Sometimes without warning, most often without a particular reason, when the individual is relaxing or even asleep, hits and can even occur. Popular panic attacks occur. A panic disorder can be a one-time occurrence, but many people usually experience repeated symptoms over a longer lifetime. The majority (66.5, i.e., 0.5 percent) of people who ever had a PA had repeated PAs. Most people recover without treatment, and only a few of them develop panic disorders from panic attacks. PAs have a lifetime prevalence of 13.2 percent (i.e. 0.1%)[18]. Repeated panic attacks also trigger a complex situation in which the person feels threatened before. A panic attack may also occur as parts of a separate illness, such as panic disorder, social phobia, or depression. Depending on the relationship between the occurrence of the attack and the lack or presence of situational stimuli, panic attacks can be classified as follows:

Sudden (untested) panic attacks are the most common type of attack in the PD in which the occurrence of a panic attack is not related to a cause of a situation (occurs suddenly as a lightning strike).

Panic attacks that occur almost often immediately after contact, or the anticipation of a trigger situation (e.g., an immediate panic attack is often caused by seeing a snake or dog) are situation-induced (triggered).

Panic attacks that are highly expected to occur when exposed to the trigger scenario, but are not inseparably connected to the trigger, and do not occur immediately after exposure (e.g., panic attacks are more likely to occur during the ride, but people frequently drive and do not have panic attacks, or they occur half an hour after the ride).

Other types of attacks include minimal symptoms that arise in a specific emotional context and night attacks.

Situational-induced attacks are more typical of social and real phobias. Situationally predisposed panic attacks are highly common in panic disorders and occur in actual and social phobias. For panic disorder diagnosis, the onset of sudden panic attacks is significant with or without agoraphobia. The frequency and severity of panic attacks vary widely. For instance, some individuals have intermediate-frequency attacks (e.g., once a week) that occur for months regularly. Others record frequent short-term (day, week) attacks separated over a long period (weeks or months) without seizures or uncommon (two per month) attacks over a long period. In panic disorders, episodes with limited symptoms are very common (e.g., similar to total panic attacks but with less related symptoms).

Chapter 1

YOU ARE THE CURE

W hen we set out on this trip, the very first thing to be mindful of is that it's all right not to feel okay. That's the starting point. You should finally take the toll of all the months or years that fear has been with you. It could have been a long time before you felt like yourself.

The cocktail of stress hormones constantly bombards a person who experiences recurrent panic attacks or general anxiety. Not only does this bombardment make your nervous system particularly susceptible to stress, but it also leaves you feeling cut off from the globe. The truth may have gone a little weird, but that's all right. You will start to feel more and more relaxed with it now that you know the discomfort you feel is actually due to your body's stress response.

The second thing to be mindful of is that you don't have an anxiety disorder as a frail or cowardly person. I've been working with some of the bravest people that you would ever hope to meet. Police officers, firefighters, and military members who were able to perform remarkably heroic feats in the line of duty and yet were tormented while off duty by anxiety issues. I served with a police chief once, a decorated officer supervising over 300 police officers, who could not wait for a haircut in the barbers. He dealt with highly pressurized conditions every working day and felt very much in control, but he felt out of control in the barber's chair as he had a panic attack there once before. So, just because you suffer from anxiety, don't think of yourself as being vulnerable or less brave than others; far from that.

I assure you that the anxiety you feel is not that different from the anxiety faced by all the other individuals who have used this technique successfully. I have come through such a broad spectrum of anxiety disorders over the years that nothing shocks me anymore. Panic disorder, generalized anxiety disorder, social anxiety, OCD, Pure O: the same thing, anxiety, is behind all the various forms.

I don't like sub categorizing anxiety into individual labels or even labeling it a disorder. "I only listed those words above so that you're clear on what's going on."

What you've heard is what I'm talking about. Labels are only useful for describing an experience that a person is experiencing right at that moment in life. They should not be interpreted as something that now constitutes a person's personality or as something that they will forever have.

People appear to over-identify with psychiatric labels until their doctor, or mental health professional has provided them with one. Yet, much like a time of sorrow or depression, an anxiety disorder is simply an emotion that a person goes through. Should we offer a mark for life to a person with a broken heart or someone suffering from grief? No, but often individuals who go through a phase of anxiety end up thinking that this diagnosis, this mark, is now part of who they are.

Chapter 2

THE DARE RESPONSE

In the United States, anxiety is the most prevalent mental health issue, affecting around 40 million individuals. You are not alone if you struggle with anxiety. There's support available. Anxiety also leaves you feeling frightened and out of control. Sweating, shaking, chest pain, racing thoughts, or trouble breathing may be experienced. People also describe anxiety as "feeling like they are going to die." Trying to combat anxiety is our immediate response to this threat. The more you battle these emotions ironically, the more powerful the anxiety becomes. A fresh and simple way to break free from anxiety and panic attacks is the DARE answer, developed by Barry McDonagh.

A four-step method includes DARE: Defuse, Allow, Run-toward, and Engage. DARE's purpose is to improve the way you handle your anxiety, making the feeling more manageable.

The steps proceed as follows:

Phase 1: Defuse

There is always fear coming out of nowhere, which can be frightening. Like a wave, anxiety is. Anxiety occurs, peaks, and then goes down slowly. Although anxiety often comes down, we prefer to think about the thoughts of "what if" arising from anxiety. What if it doesn't stop this feeling "or" what if I have a public panic attack "or" what if I lose my job? The anxiety is fed by these feelings, making it more intense. Tell yourself, "So what?" instead of telling yourself the "what ifs," Tell yourself, "What, then??" "My heart is really strong and I'm going to get through this as I always have" or "so what?" in the past. Someone will support me in two minutes if I have a public panic attack. These questions change, teaching you to react to the fear in a constructive way.

Phase 2: Allow

This move helps you to accept and encourage anxiety to take place actively. Your fear isn't outrunning you, but you have to step with it. Getting comfortable with being uncomfortable is the secret to the DARE answer. Life is full of unpleasant experiences, so learning how to be present is crucial. The anxiety you feel may be unpleasant, but in fact, it's just an excitement aimed at shielding you from your nervous system but just in the wrong way. With a new approach to the excitement, it then inevitably starts to slip down. A simple way to make this move is to say to yourself over and over again, "I embrace and allow this nervous feeling." You may not believe it at first, but you will eventually. This move is also the toughest because pain is difficult to embrace. With practice, though, you will come to see the outcomes that it has.

Phase 3: Run toward

You must run towards it to break the misconception that your anxiety is a dangerous threat! As I said before, anxiety is just your nervous system's excitement. There are almost similar physiological stimuli and reactions to fear and excitement, but the difference is in our perception. For instance, if you were in the woods and heard the bushes rustle, if you thought it was a wild tiger compared to a fluffy kitten, you would respond very differently. The triggers stay the same (the rustling bushes), but your reaction shifts the interpretation of what feline will leap out at you. This illusion of a threat will end by moving to a more optimistic view of your anxiety. When you start feeling nervous, say to yourself over again, "I'm excited about this feeling." Instead of trying to combat it, sprint towards the nervous feeling. This comment will alter the way your brain and body react to anxiety.

Phase 4: Engage

Anxiety will always look for a way to pull you back in, so to calm down completely, it is important to find a task that you can interact with. While it is nice to find a diversion, it is not as effective as completely engaging in an activity that gets your mind's attention. Watching TV or reading, for example, is also a diversion because it engages the mind's resources. Completing a job task or performing an exercise of mindfulness removes the energy you have from fear and uses it in a different place. If a job that distracts you instead of engaging you is easier to do at first, then start there. Then you can switch to more engaging tasks until you become more secure with your DARE responses.

Do not forget that you have strength! Anxiety does not make you a bad person but makes you human instead. In your battle against anxiety, you are not alone. Know that the secret is you. Recovery is focused on your capacity to embrace your distressing thoughts and emotions and accept them. The aim is not to fully end these nervous feelings but to end the anxiety and allow it to happen. All that it takes to desensitize your mind and body is a better reaction.

PANIC ATTACKS!

Chapter 3

THE DARE RESPONSE FOR PANIC ATTACK

Depending on the present life situation, a person with general anxiety may score between a 5 and a 7 on a scale of 1 to 10 (where 10 is the highest). They have what's known as a panic attack when the person tops the scale around an 8 or a 9. There are experiences with very extreme anxiety. If you've ever seen one, you would remember. They're memorable enough!

The fight-or-flight answer is a false cause for panic attacks. A sort of catastrophic thought that says, "This could just kill me," is at the center of panic attacks.

Unexpectedly, panic attacks come on and typically involve any of the following feelings or experiences:

- Sensations of shortness of breath or smothering
- Pounding heart
- Paresthesias (numbness or tingling sensations)
- Shaking
- Sweating
- Nausea/tummy cramps
- Chest pain
- Feeling dizzy or unsteady
- An out-of-body or unreal feeling
- Shivers or hot flushes

- Feeling of choking

We have our first panic attack, we are immediately afraid of it happening again and start avoiding situations that could trigger it. The fear of fear sets in and spinning begins the anxiety loop.

Let me begin by saying that if you suffer from panic attacks, you need to remember that you are safe, no matter how scary it feels. There'll be no harm coming to you. You will not suffocate or die. It's not dangerous, even though it's very unpleasant.

There is an ancient Chinese term that translates as a "paper tiger," known as zhilaohu. It refers to anything that appears aggressive but is ineffective and unable to withstand challenges. A paper tiger, terrifying but ultimately harmless, is exactly what a panic attack is. (See the chapter "Give Up Fearing These Sensations" for a more detailed discussion on why these sensations are not dangerous during a panic attack.)

About panic attacks, Dr. Harry Barry, an Irish medical practitioner, and mental health specialist have this to say:

The role of your stress system is not to destroy you but to keep you safe and alive. The symptoms of anxiety are painful but not dangerous. As a doctor, you have my word — this adrenaline rush will not kill you.

It's important to remember that you are not the enemy of panic attacks; they are the result of trying to keep yourself safe. It's your ancient mechanism for biological protection that pumps you full of stress hormones so you can fight or flee from a perceived threat. When we needed to avoid sabre-toothed tigers thousands of years ago, this mechanism worked well. Still, when it's activated while stuck in traffic or traveling on the subway, it's significantly less helpful.

Think of all the panic attacks that you had when the fear peaked and terrified you. It settled back down again right when you felt you couldn't bear it anymore. Don't forget, 100 percent has been the track record so far for getting through panic attacks. That is pretty good.

Remember, in waves, fear arrives. A very big wave can arrive now and then (a.k.a. a panic attack), but if you don't react correctly in the first few moments, anxiety will swamp you, leaving you rattled and afraid of the next one.

The key to ending panic attacks is to take the anxiety away from the emotions you are having. You need to sprint from the fear with greater intensity when faced with a panic attack. As explained in the previous chapter, you do so by getting excited by the nervous arousal, and then you ask for anxiety to produce more.

PANIC ATTACKS!

Chapter 4

I THINK, THEREFORE, I FEAR

Anxiety is not a psychiatric disorder. Your brain is not fractured. You are not going to go nuts. I'm not just saying this to make you feel better; I am saying it because it's real. Not how it feels mentally, the worst thing about anxiety, but rather the sly way it makes you believe you're abnormal. One of the most common experiences with anxiety is feeling abnormal. Almost everybody begins to fear their sanity after experiencing high anxiety and stress hormones for a few months.

I bet you've felt like you're the only person in the world feeling the way you do at some point.

I know no one has these kinds of bizarre thoughts and emotions, so I have to be furious, don't I?

YOU ARE NOT YOUR ANXIETY

By now, you'll have gathered that normalizing fear as much as possible is a crucial element of The DARE Answer to avoid its vicious cycle. Part of the normalization is having to understand that your fear is NOT yours. Only thoughts and nothing more are the nervous thoughts you feel. The real you, they don't represent. They result from the interaction of stress hormones with your vigilant and imaginative mind. You're not the only individual going through this journey, too. Note, about 40 million American adults alone (about one in six of the population) suffer from any form of anxiety disorder at any given time, according to the National Institute of Mental Health.

Translate those numbers, and you know that you're not alone, as you feel alienated from your anxiety, and your experience is normal. Focus on the 'one in six' figure while you're out and about. You may have thought that no one else could cope with your specific anguish, but look again. The woman preparing breakfast for you could be fending off an attack of panic. The frustrated man at the bank in front of you might hate the claustrophobic feeling of waiting in line. A mother driving an SUV may be afraid she'll have a panic attack with a car full of kids on the highway.

Anxiety is such a prevalent problem, but no one speaks freely about it. A taboo subject is still the issue of mental wellbeing. Our celebrities happily chat about their colon cleansing or their sex lives on national TV, but their mental well-being is rarely discussed. It seems that this is too intimate, the subject too fragile.

Alprazolam (the generic name for Xanax), with over 50 million annual prescriptions written for only one antianxiety drug, isn't it time we started talking more honestly about anxiety in particular and how common and natural an emotion it is? If the mass media were able to normalize society's entire experience, I believe far fewer people will fall into the nervous pit of fearful fear.

A DOUBLE LIFE

Did anxiety make you lead a double life? I risk a guess that you pretend to the outside world that all is fine when inside you fear that you may lose your mind. You're guarding this secret against the world, a little like a secret agent. I bet that very few people will even believe you have an anxiety disorder at all. Isn't it incredible how we can constantly represent the world with one picture when we feel tormented inside? Women are fantastic at that, but men are the great masters of fear tucked away. I know it all because I used to be one of those secret agents, too.

When I was going through an extremely difficult time with my anxiety, someone once commented that I seemed as laid back as a duck floating down a creek. What they never knew was that this duck was paddling like crazy under the water just to remain upright. I coached a very well-known TV presenter a few years ago who was troubled by the fear of getting a panic attack live on TV. He was afraid that his superiors could suspect something, so he walked into the studio every day, smiling and behaving as if nothing could faze him. For years, he kept all of his doubts and anxieties to himself. He didn't even tell his wife that he was going through the constant torture every time he went on air.

I bet you are an unbelievable actor. You pretend to the world that all is all right and then secretly spend the day dodging and spinning any scenario that could make you nervous. That double life is strenuous. You may have one or two close friends who suspect anything because you often avoid those scenarios, but the rest of the people in your life don't suspect anything, by and wide.

A clear example of how well people mask their worries is flight. Statistics indicate that about 30% of all passengers on any given flight are nervous about flying and about 10% are highly anxious. Still, during a flight, it is difficult to find those 10 percent. They sit close and secretly grip on their armrests, all without making a peep until their knuckles turn white. They go through absolute terror, but because of even greater fear, the fear of shame, they mask it well—the anxiety of embarrassment.

Anxiety and shame can play together in an almost comical way. Let's assume you're having lunch with some work colleagues, for instance. Your heart unexpectedly skips a beat, and your chest tightens. You persuade yourself that you're going to have a heart attack in a split second, but instead of telling them to call an ambulance, you're politely excusing yourself and running for the toilet. You would rather die alone in a toilet cubicle from cardiac arrest than create a scene.

Whenever you put the fear of embarrassment above your fear of imminent death, I think you will find that anxiety is definitely at play!

Chapter 5

ARE YOU ANXIOUS? ...OR DEPRESSED?

People interchangeably use "stress" and "anxiety" in popular parlance. Also, groups for mental health appear to lump the two together.

For example, the Anxiety and Depression Association of America (ADAA) has tools to help people handle "anxiety and stress." But to find an explanation for how the two vary, it takes some searching on the ADAA Site, and that explanation is also unhelpfully brief: "Stress is a reaction to a danger in a situation." Anxiety is a response to pressure.

"There is no universal consensus on how to contrast these two principles, even among psychiatrists and psychologists," says Richard Maddock, MD, a psychiatry and behavioral sciences professor at the University of California, Davis. While both stress and anxiety can cause similar reactions in the human body, reactions associated with several health problems, including depression and heart disease, Maddock says they are not the same.

He says stress is a wider term than anxiety. Stress may be both physical or psychological and either positive or bad. Maddock refers to exercise as a type of physical stress that can contribute to positive changes while challenging the body. Likewise, certain individuals relish the short-term tension associated with public appearances or other pressure-packed circumstances.

On the other hand, fear is always mentally induced and, he notes, always uncomfortable. There are three vital components of anxiety. The first is a perception, actual or imagined, of some form of threat. (The danger may be a turbulent flight or just the possibility of a turbulent flight.) The second aspect, Maddock says, is "a sense that the threat needs to be resolved or something to do about it." The third is "a sense that the ability to respond appropriately to the threat is missing." This feeling of helplessness is important; when people feel prepared to face a challenge or threat, the threat is important.

Another useful way to distinguish between the two is to think of stress as something that is exacerbated by an external obstacle while anxiety is born in mind. "Gerard Sanacora, PhD, MD, a psychiatry professor at Yale School of Medicine, says:" stress is something that pushes the body or mind away from homeostasis or its normal set point. That something could be a raging toddler, a workplace disaster, or a bear just wandering into your campsite. Stress may cause a pounding heart, sweaty hands, jitteriness, or other short-lived physiological reactions designed to help an individual respond to these kinds of external challenges.

"It is impossible to make the lives of people with less traumatic incidents. But you can adjust the way certain incidents are viewed, which can reduce anxiety."

Meanwhile, anxiety is the mind and body's persistent response to — or anticipation of — an external threat or stressor, Sanacora says. If you're concerned that a crisis could arise at work or a bear could wander into your campsite, you're experiencing anxiety, not stress. "You can have anxiety without any external event," Sanacora says. This is a big deal because even if the external threat never materializes, anxiety can trigger all the same internal responses associated with stress-related health issues. Anxiety can make your heart rate speed up, your palms sweat, and your mind race with worry. It can also flood your blood with stress-related hormones like adrenaline and cortisol.

"In many ways, anxiety is the experiential component of stress, and it's dependent on how a person perceives that external source of stress," Sanacora says. If a teacher surprises two students with a pop quiz, the external source of stress — the quiz — is the same for both. But if one of those students has studied the quiz material and the other has not — or if one cares more about their grades than the other — the anxiety each person experiences will be quite different.

Why does any of this matter? "It's hard to make people's lives have fewer stressful events," Sanacora says. "But you can change the way they perceive those events, which can reduce anxiety." Lowering anxiety helps limit the hormonal, immune, and nervous system reactions associated with an increased risk for stress-related diseases, he says. And recognizing the psychological underpinnings of anxiety can help people learn to sidestep or calm the unhealthy internal processes it triggers. This is true whether a person is grappling with ordinary anxiety or an anxiety disorder.

One way to temper anxiety is to confront its source. For example, someone who feels anxious about speaking in public could enroll in an improv class. Or a person with a fear of dogs could spend time with a friendly pooch. Exposure therapy of this sort has proved effective in treating a range of anxiety disorders. And it's just one type of cognitive-behavioral therapy, which is broadly defined as teaching a person to think about the source of their anxiety in new and less worrisome ways.

"One of the main points here is that all people experience stress, but not all stress produces anxiety," Sanacora says. Anxiety is the fuel that keeps the fires of stress burning. Take away the fuel, and the fire burns out.

PANIC ATTACKS!

Chapter 6

DO YOU HAVE AN ANXIETY DISORDER?

You may have an anxiety disorder if you experience signs of anxiety for a long period.

Why do I feel nervous and panicky?

Read, for more information about symptoms.

Anxiety Disorder Generalized (GAD)

Generalized anxiety disorder (GAD) is a long-term illness that, rather than one particular case, can make you feel nervous about a wide variety of circumstances and problems.

Maybe you have GAD if:

- Your insecurity is uncontrollable and triggers anxiety;

- Your problems affect your everyday life, including education, work, and social life;

- You will not put your problems behind;

- You are worried about all types of things, such as your career or wellbeing, and trivial problems, such as household chores;

If anxiety is impacting your daily life or causing you pain, you can see your GP. Based on your symptoms, they will diagnose your disease, which may include:

- Restless or on the verge feeling;

- Being irritable;

- Quickly get tired;

- Having trouble focusing or feeling like the mind goes blank;

- Having trouble getting to sleep or remaining asleep;

- Getting muscles which are stressed...

There is counseling available if you are diagnosed with GAD.

Other types of anxiety disorder

Several other forms of anxiety disorder exist, including:

- Panic disorder-a condition in which you have recurrent, daily panic attacks;

- Phobias-an intense or unreasonable fear, such as an animal or a spot, of something;

- Agoraphobia-many phobias associated with conditions such as leaving home, being in crowds, or traveling alone;

- Obsessive-compulsive disorder is a disease that normally includes intrusive thoughts or desires and repetitive actions;

- Post-traumatic stress disorder-a condition triggered by things that are terrifying or distressing...

Chapter 7

GIVE UP SAVING NO TO ANXIETY

The second stage is one of the toughest steps for most people in Chapter 2 "The DARE Response": the concept of lowering resistance and just facilitating and embracing the anxiety. This chapter aims to help you accomplish that by helping you move with each nervous wave of anxiety more thoroughly.

This great dog named Shadow used to be in my family. It was a cross between a collie and a black Labrador. He used to sit in the front room of our house all day long, waiting for someone to come to the front door. If anyone had arrived, he would have gone completely bonkers!

Before ... we invited the person in.

Shadow would bounce off the walls, barking loudly with all the hair on his back standing straight up, if we kept the person at the door (for example, the FedEx guy). He wouldn't listen, no matter how hard we tried to tell him to lie down and stop barking.

His reasoning was: "I am the guard of this building, and if a person is not invited by my owner, then that person is undesirable and therefore a threat."

I used to hold friends at the door for a couple of minutes sometimes and then let them in (if they were brave enough), just to see the difference in Shadow's response. Each time, it was the same. As soon as they had gone through the front door, he would immediately stop barking and sit down in his seat.

Anxiety is much like a dog with a guard. Your protector, he is. It's the emotional part of the brain that activates your fight-or-flight response, built to keep you from harm. The owner (your logical brain) wants you to convince him that the odd bodily stimuli that visit you are not a real danger and that everything is all right.

But just thinking, as we've seen, "Everything's all right." "Calm down right now," doesn't work. Much like Shadow, anxiety reacts to your acts much better. Mentally, you need to let the fear in. Your emotional brain feels that the danger is real, and there is something to be afraid of if you keep the door closed on fear. Your emotional brain (your guard dog) backs off and calms down when you invite your nervous sensations in with complete approval of them.

Charlotte Joko Beck says, "*We have to face the pain we've been running from, we just need to learn to rest in it and let it turn us with its searing strength.*"

I love the way Beck communicates what is at the very heart of true acceptance: to rest in it and let its searing force transforms us.

The way you cure it is to learn to relax in pain. Resting in painful feelings provides an opportunity for the mind and body to relax and detoxify from the stress reaction. "So, instead of putting it aside, when you feel fear or anxiety emerge, whisper to yourself," It's okay. "Give the moment and what you feel a gentle" yes. Acceptance of anxiety offers a sense of calm and acceptance that, in time, will be all right.

Nobody needs to be worried. Who would? Who would? It's a truly awkward, disturbing experience. But not having to feel anxiety will not make things any easier or make it go away. All that comes from wishing things were different than they are, is anger and tension. The way you're feeling right now is the way it is. Your fear doesn't have to love you. You just have to approve it.

"*Acceptance is a pre-condition of change*", Dr. Carl Rogers wrote. Acceptance of the current situation is your liberation from it since it enables a meaningful change to occur. Saying "*yes*" to anxiety opens you up to the motivation and resilience behind the anxiety so that you can turn it into something positive from something fearful.

"I embrace this nervous feeling and allow it"

You improve your tolerance to nervous stimuli when you say "yes" in this way. The tension you experience is diminished and gradually removed with this increased tolerance. You end up with what you want as a side effect. You end up feeling peaceful. It is not because you pushed it away that the anxiety leaves, but because you no longer fuel it with resistance and terror. "The very heart of The DARE Answer is to say "yes.

Please don't assume that giving in or surrendering to it is about saying "yes "to anxiety. Saying "yes" is not subjugation but a statement of empowerment. It's about you calling a civil war ceasefire that you've been waging against yourself. To tell "yes" comes from the deep and grounded you.

I know that the idea of saying "yes "to anxiety is easy to agree with, but it is much harder to enforce. If you use this strategy, as you engage with your anxiety, you have to pay attention to your thinking processes. Many people think they're saying "yes" when they're still saying "no," in fact. They're willing to take a few small steps towards anxiety, but they're afraid of it swamping them and thus holding back and never really doing it 100%.

Let me send you the example of Christine, with whom I recently talked. A lump in her throat and dizzy sensations are her nervous feelings. She's afraid that when she's outside her house, she could faint, even though she's never fainted before.

She said to me, "I'm trying to stop anxiety with your approach, but it doesn't really work." It doesn't go away. What am I doing incorrectly? I called her attention to her choice of words: "Trying to avoid fear with your approach ... It's not going anywhere."

I clarified that she must avoid saying 'no' to the fear and ease herself into the nervous discomfort to do The DARE Answer correctly.

She can't hide from it, or she can't try to stop it. In Christine's case, that implies that she must go to the places where these sensations manifest (in her case at the shopping mall) and sit with them there, not drive them away, but become their observer and get comfortable in the anxious discomfort. I clarified to Christine that it is not approval of them to drive these sensations away or attempt to "make them stop."

All-day long, she needs to encourage them to be present and say "yes" to the anxiety. Lump in the throat, come on!

Let's go and shop. Oh, you're coming with us too, dizzy spells! You shift yourself out of battle or flight as you participate and become mates. That is what it means to say "yes."

That prevents the inner tension and allows the waves of anxiety you feel to flow with your thoughts and emotions. It's not a matter of pretending to enjoy the sensations. It's about keeping an open mind towards them and welcoming them. This mentality helps you go to places now and always have a nice time, regardless of whether the sensations are there.

Initially, Christine found it difficult to embrace the sensations because she thought letting them in would just make them get worse. Perhaps you're feeling the same way? You may be afraid that welcoming you in and making friends with the thing that frightens you will only cause you to go over the edge. This is where you are going to have to trust me and this process. You've endured the worst bouts of anxiety already. What's been going on since then is that you keep your fear locked in place with your resistance to it. The quicksand that holds you trapped in this resistance. You gradually pull yourself out of the muck as you stop saying 'no' and drop the resistance.

The process of embracing anxiety, I believe, is a bit like learning not to scratch an itch that irritates you. The itch is all you can think about initially, and you keep going back to scratch it for some relief. Of course, scratching the itch just makes it worse, and so you become obsessed with the discomfort it gives you. Via acceptance, you finally learn to sit without rubbing it with the pain of the itch. You concentrate on your day and, without scratching it, encourage the itch to be there. Especially in the early stages, it's not easy to do, but eventually, the itch begins to be less of an irritant, and you feel it less and less until it's gone.

When you accept and stop fighting the fear, the same thing occurs. You don't react to it negatively anymore. Eventually, the brain filters it out, and you do not feel its existence anymore. You stop fueling it and set yourself free from its discomfort as soon as you stop reacting to it in terror.

It is not because you will never again have nervous sensations. From time to time, they will manifest, particularly when you're stressed or tired, but now you have a default way of responding to them. To it, you say "yes. I have already referred to the fact that combating fear with your anxiety is like playing a tug-of-war. The more the fear pushes out, the more you pull against it. The tension and friction you feel come from the rope that is so tightly held by you. You're afraid to let it go, just in case you lose the battle. You lower the rope and the resistance by learning to say "yes" to the fear.

Chapter 8

GIVE UP FEARING THESE SENSATIONS

A fear of stimuli fuels anxiety and panic. You need to avoid obsessing and fearing the anxious thoughts and feelings that scare you to get out of an anxious state. I include physical sensations, such as a beating heart or a tight chest, in this chapter on sensations and mental sensations, such as repetitive thoughts or de-realization.

By shedding light on the most common sensations associated with anxiety, I want to help you give up your fear of sensations and demonstrate how you can apply The DARE Answer to them. I want to stress the importance of calming your reaction to these sensations during and then learning to relax in the nervous discomfort they cause.

Remember: healing is never about stimuli being absent. When you enter a stage where sensations manifest, complete recovery is, and you pay them no attention. You should go about your day-to-day life and not think about whether or not they are there. That's when anxiety is not a concern for you anymore. Then, you see that there is no fear in the sensations; it is in your resistance to the sensations.

Let me have an example for you. After we've played, we don't get worried about a beating heart because we know the workout was the source of the feeling. After having stubbed a foot, we do not get nervous either. When we can't find a reason for the feeling, the issue comes. To keep us secure, our brains are built to keep a vigilant lookout for threats. We prefer to leap to fearful conclusions if we experience a strange feeling and don't know why it manifests.

Just to send you an instance of that, scratch your head right now with your fingertips. Listen carefully to the noise that it makes. Now, imagine that you don't know what triggers the sound. Wouldn't you start to worry that there was something wrong going on in your head? The higher your level of general anxiety, the more unknown stimuli you overreact to.

Another example I want to give is a man who told me that he once took his wife's car to work and got into a panic when he suddenly felt a very odd feeling in his feet, an example of how our minds race to fill in the gaps. He was feeling very nervous at the time, and this odd sensation caused a panic attack to start. He then looked down to see that the car's air conditioning was set up with the cold ventilation pointed at his feet. The air provoked an odd feeling. For the first time, he burst out laughing and realized how oversensitive he was too odd bodily sensations. It stresses that anxiety is not in the sensations; it is in our resistance to certain sensations or reactions to them.

I'm going to show you how to apply The DARE Answer so that, regardless of whether you know the source of those sensations or not, you can have a non-anxious response to any bodily sensations.

You can very well find yourself feeling them to some degree as you read about each sensation in this chapter. If that's the case, don't worry, welcome them, on the other side. You have an opportunity to practice getting the right attitude toward them only when these sensations are present.

I have described some of the common sensations linked to anxiety and panic below. These are common criminals, but there are several more that you may meet that are not described here. You can nevertheless get a very good idea of how to apply The DARE Answer to them by reading through the examples given if you have sensations that are not described here. You don't have to read through, and an example is given in this and the following chapter ('Give Up Fearing These Situations'). You can skip ahead to those that are most important to you. I'll go through each of them after every feeling and explain how the DARE Answer works in that particular situation. It goes without saying that your doctor can examine any feeling that causes you to concern in order to rule out potential causes other than anxiety. Not only is it necessary from a medical point of view to do so, but it can also help minimize nervous thoughts that something more severe may be incorrect.

PHYSICAL SENSATIONS

- Heart Sensations: Palpitations and Missed; Heartbeats/Fainting/Passing Out;
- Breathing Anxiety;
- Nausea/Fear of Vomiting, Fainting/Passing Out;
- Choking Sensations/Tight Throat;
- Blurred Vision;
- Headaches;
- Shaking/Tremors;
- Tingling Sensations;
- Weak Legs/Jelly Legs...

MENTAL SENSATIONS

- Disturbing Thoughts;
- Depression;
- Fear of "Going Crazy";
- Unreality/Depersonalization;
- Losing Control...

PHYSICAL SENSATIONS

HEART SENSATIONS

At some point, most people who have suffered panic attacks fear for the wellbeing of their souls. If you are concerned about heart attacks, if for nothing more than to put your mind to rest and could the impact of nervous "what if" thinking, you should definitely have your heart health checked out.

If you get a clean health bill, trust the outcomes, and don't second-assess them. Get a second opinion if you really have to, but after that, stop doubting your good health.

Breathlessness and chest pain are the main signs of heart failure and mild palpitations and fainting. In general, such symptoms are related to the amount of physical activity performed, i.e., the more you exercise, the worse the symptoms get.

PALPITATIONS

Palpitations are brief, rapid times during which the heart unexpectedly begins to beat rapidly. This can ring warning bells if you are in a sensitive condition because you fear a sudden heart attack. The more you fear, the more your heart beats faster. Therefore, it is understandable that you might leap to conclusions and call for medical assistance in this case. You need to know that palpitations are normal and can often be induced by fatigue or caffeine-like stimulants. Your heart is an extremely powerful muscle, and it won't stop or burst just because it's pounding fast and hard. All-day long, a healthy heart will beat fast and not be in any danger.

MISSED HEARTBEATS

Extra systoles are the medical term for skipped cardiac beats. The effect of an extra beat between two natural beats is typically a missing heartbeat. It can appear as if one beat has been missed due to the delay that accompanies this extra beat. The next normal heartbeat will sound like a bit of a jolt since the lower chambers of the heart fill during the pause with a greater-than-usual volume of blood. You sometimes freeze when you feel this feeling and wait in fear to see if your heart is in danger.

Such missing beats are harmless in general. Sitting down when you feel this feeling might help, but if you want to keep going, do so. Exercise will not cause the problem to get worse, and do not persuade yourself that the only way to help the situation is to go home to lie down. Your actions will reinforce the negative idea that your home is the only safe place to be if you withdraw every time you experience an odd sensation. Your heart is not an atomic clock that has to keep time flawless at all times. This accelerates; it slows down. It sometimes beats unusually. You can note an odd beat or two from time to time. It's nothing to be mad about.

Research by Dr. Harold Kennedy was recently published by the New England Journal of Medicine, which found that healthy people with repeated irregular heartbeats tend to be no more vulnerable than the general population to heart attacks. The majority of even the healthiest individuals experience chest palpitations, missing beats, or banging.

You can persuade yourself that it can somehow get confused and forget how to beat correctly if you worry enough about your heart or focus too hard on its actions. It is very normal for people suffering from this form of anxiety to check their pulse at regular intervals to make sure it is beating correctly. You need to be mindful that your conscious mind can't stop your heart from pounding, no matter how much you think about it. All it can do is accelerate it through fear and anxiety for a while or slow it down slightly through calming mental exercises.

Chapter 9

GIVE UP FEARING THESE SITUATIONS

So how did you go from being scared of going shopping or sitting and getting your hair cut to having nothing bothering you? You are knowledgeable and proficient; you have traveled far and wide. So why do you suddenly have to white-knuckle your way through daily circumstances that have never before caused you anxiety?

The response is fairly straightforward. You were frightened of nervous feelings in your body. The fear has shaken your confidence in the capacity of your body to control itself in some circumstances. It's never just the situation you're dealing with-it's yourself.

This lack of faith doesn't take place immediately. One day, you didn't wake up unexpectedly; unable to do all these stuff you're afraid of now. It was a slow process of anxiety that, bit by bit, eroded your confidence. It is also possible to trace such fears back to one incident. Perhaps, for example, you were in a line and had a manifestation of nervous feeling. The experience was enough to scare you, and you started avoiding lines from that moment on. Or you may have been caught in traffic and suffered your first panic attack. Then your mind makes the connection that driving is something to be scared of, so now you're afraid of driving and start avoiding it:

- Avoidance creeps in this easy way. We feel some relief when we initially avoid situations, and that relief from discomfort strengthens our avoidance. The issue, though, is that avoidance is a trap-in fact. It is the death knell of liberty.

- Avoidance converts a fear of a situation into a phobia of it over time. A phobia is described as a fear of or aversion to something serious or irrational.

People suffering from anxiety can develop phobias about driving, flying, or being in enclosed spaces or crowded spaces (with no easy exit). Truly, the list is very long. It can include fear of not having a safe individual with you, fear of being out of your safe zone somewhere, etc. For about any scenario you can imagine, there's a word for clinical phobia.

Why phobias evolve is easy to understand. All this is related to a lack of faith in the capacity to tolerate anxious feelings. Due to this lack of trust, an anxious individual struggles to control their anxiety by avoiding a specific situation at all costs.

For a while, avoidance will work, but ultimately it traps you. It shrinks your life and limits it, depriving you of many things that can bring you joy. There are three steps to the standard progression of avoidance:

A. Catching a panic attack in a real situation;

B. Connecting the situation with risk;

C. Whenever possible, avoid the situation.

It never ceases to amaze me how imaginative people can become when they want to stop. I'm talking about preparing every aspect of their day to not have to leave their comfort zone and face those conditions that make them nervous. Eventually, this comfort zone becomes a jail. You need to move out of it using The DARE Answer to break free from this jail.

THE "WHAT IFS" AND TRYING TO CONTROL SITUATIONS

I will illustrate how to apply The DARE Answer in a range of real-life scenarios in the examples that follow. Since it would take so much room to go through every case, I will provide examples of the most popular ones instead. If I do not discuss a particular problem you are dealing with, by reading the examples below, you can still get a very clear understanding of how to manage it.

In essence, there are two key components of any evasion maneuver, the "what ifs" (which you are familiar with from other sections of this book) and attempting to manage situations.

The "what ifs" is the driving force behind all anxiety in situations.

What if I go shopping and find myself overwhelmed?

What if I get on the plane and there's too much pressure for me to deal with?

What if I lose control and, in front of others I know, do something humiliating?

What ifs "are the sparks that, if they are allowed to, ignite the flame of fear and anxiety in situations." An anxious individual will try to monitor circumstances to minimize the influence of the "what ifs."

They will worry about it for days or even weeks in advance if they have to face a situation that they associate with fear and anxiety. To get them through it, they can need the help of a crutch, such as a safe person or medicine. The nervous individual will also prepare an 'out' when they have to face such a situation.

Typical "outs" include:

Sitting on the outside of a row of seats to quickly reach the exit, pretending to receive a significant call if you feel the need to bailout

Always drive your car so that you never have to wait for a ride home or sit in the passenger seat of another person's car.

Still knowing where the bathroom is in case you have to go unexpectedly or just have to be alone for a while

Do have a cell near at hand in case you need to call for assistance.

Trying to manage circumstances in this way is as unhelpful as preventing them because you are always sending the message to yourself that when, of course, you are not, you are in possible danger. A panic attack will not kill you. On a lonely island of fear and anxiety, you are as completely healthy as sitting in a hospital surrounded by doctors. So realize that you aren't physiologically in any more danger at Walmart than you are at home. You can see that what you have to master in the end is yourself as you come to truly understand this, not the situation. The fear is not in the situation; it's in your reaction to the emotions in the situation that you have.

You're going to learn below how in multiple circumstances to develop a greater tolerance of nervous stimuli. In circumstances that make you nervous, learning to feel secure and safe is the key to overcoming your anxiety. In several cases, the DARE Answer may be used.

Chapter 10

GIVE UP FEARING ANXIOUS THOUGHTS

The world around us can't be controlled; we can only control our reaction to it.

'Stress' is our modern life's buzzword. All that the media seems to speak about is tension. Anything done to us is this tension. We are given the message that we are all victims of stress because of the fast-paced world we now live in.

Nobody thinks about terror anymore. It's a word that's almost out of fashion in the counseling community, and I think that's a shame. I like the word "worry" a lot because it represents a more precise image of what is going on inside our minds and hearts.

General anxiety, triggered by worry, is not caused by stress. Since we are concerned, we are anxious. We're not worried, but to stop getting the house repossessed, we have to drop the children off, go to work, and make a living. Because of the way we worry about all of those things, we are anxious. We wouldn't be worried if we didn't care about all of it.

If we can start talking about anxiety again, the situation would be better clarified. It puts back in our minds the blame for what's happening to us. There is less space for the world to blame for doing this to us and more room for us to look at our world reaction.

In this book, every single piece of advice is based on the idea that you, the reader, are responsible for your destiny and that you should take steps personally in your own life to put an end to your anxiety. That's why, because worry is something you can become conscious of and then act to improve, I prefer to talk about worry.

The driving force of general anxiety is worry. Currently, 'to strangle' is the root of the term concern. When we worry, we strangle and contract our lives. We are worried because we believe that doing so will fix our issues and allow us to feel more in control, but it cuts us off from life.

I want to speak about the two forms of concern that affect individuals in this chapter. The fear of objects and the fear of feelings.

The anxiety about things is clear. We are worried about our health, our loved ones' health, money, relationships, careers. We're also concerned if, after we left the house, we switched off the oven.

The second type of concern is the one that only individuals with anxiety suffer from. It's about thinking about feelings. Those are questions about the way we think and the feelings that we have. Why can't I stop worrying about bizarre stuff like that? "A form of concern. The second kind of concern will turn on top of itself and trigger our thoughts to fear a vicious loop. To deal with both types of worries, you can use The DARE Answer.

Let's take a closer look at these two types of anxiety.

Worry Over Things

"Our primary business is not to see what lies dimly at a distance, but to do what is obviously at hand."

I doubt that someone who doesn't know what it's like to worry is alive. We've transformed fear into an art form in the West. We're concerned about small things like, "Am I going to get to the appointment on time?" Serious things like,

"*How am I going to live when I'm out of work now*?" Everyone has different forms of anxiety, and it's all about the person going through it.

What can seem to one person like a tragedy can seem to another like a trivial matter. At the deepest level, concern about belonging is the one worry that almost every human being suffers. Would my peers/family/society embrace me? Am I going to be loved? You first need to ask yourself frankly if you're ready to give it up before exploring how to handle the concern. Maybe you want to keep worrying because you feel you need it?

Many individuals are reluctant to let go of anxiety because they fear that they will succumb to any threat. Worry can become a habit that we believe is the only thing that keeps us protected and out of the way of harm.

We run around in a state of hysteria from one thing to the next in the mistaken belief that everything would fall apart if we slowed down for just a minute, and it would all be our fault because we dared to stop worrying. That may seem a little dramatic, but for many people, it's the truth. It's the way our nervous minds work.

Perhaps you think thinking about your job or your finances make you safer? Perhaps you think the fear of illness stops you from doing something that might cause this illness?

The truth is that you wouldn't be more or less at risk than you already are if you stopped worrying. Suddenly, you won't miss deadlines or fail to pick up the children or pay the bills. It's a fallacy to get things done; you need to be motivated by concern and fear.

You will still have the opportunity to engage the part of your brain capable of predicting future events and solving problems without concern. To become a better person, you don't need to be inspired by worry. Here's how you use The DARE Answer to worry about stuff: For starters, let's say you have a fear that a loved one may get sick.

Maybe they've been sick in the past, and now you're afraid the disease might come back.

Start by defusing the worry of "what if" each time it manifests itself. What if his disease returns?

Then how can we cope?

"Oh well, if that happens, we'll have to deal with it, but it didn't happen right now, so I'm not going to get concerned with that right now." Then, without getting upset by it, allow this concern to be present. Tell yourself that being concerned about such things is perfectly natural, and do not beat yourself up every time a "what if" thought intrudes.

The "what ifs" can continue to loop, so all the while acknowledging that such anxiety is natural to feel, you'll need to defuse them. Taking a piece of paper and writing them out repeatedly, if they loop incessantly, run towards them. This has an immediate release impact.

When that is over, get busy with something and completely concentrate your attention on what you're doing. Before the anxiety about things started, if you weren't doing something, in particular, find anything that engages your focus so that the nervous portion of your mind avoids obsessing about your fears.

Dale Carnegie wrote a wonderful book called How to Stop Worrying and Start Living on how to deal with this first aspect of concern, the "concern about things." In it, he speaks of "shutting down the iron doors of the past and the future." Live in small, day-closed compartments.

He means that we have to learn to live every day and not waste too much time dwelling on the future or the past. For instance, Regret is mostly about stuff that we've done or not done in the past, and anxiety is typically about a potential case.

Carnegie also states the fundamental importance of acceptance (the second phase of The DARE Response). You have to "be prepared to have it that way," to embrace things as they are, not as you wish they were right now. You melt the stress that worries causes by embracing the obstacles that you face in life.

We may wish for the future to be different and make plans to improve our situation if we are faced with a difficult problem, but we must first embrace reality as it is here and now. So that means that after you have endured the initial shock of that traumatic encounter, whether you have lost your job or just had a health scare, you must then step into a state of acceptance of it to move on.

Acceptance gives you the starting point from which you can move forward without bringing the extra concern to the problem. This helps you to continue to enjoy life while still facing the current challenge. But the job is getting simpler now because you are finally giving up the most tiring aspect of every real challenge, which is the constant concern about it.

The above topic refers to situations we have no power over; there are sometimes things we can act on, and taking action, in that case, can do a great amount to ease the concern.

You'll feel more in control and less nervous if there is an action you can take to resolve your concern. So, for instance, if you have just lost your work, you might take action by doing the following:

1. Write down what you are thinking about, exactly;

2. What you should do about it, write down;

3. Decide what you should do;

4. Begin to carry out the decision immediately;

If I ever find myself worrying about a matter, I decide if this concern is something about which I can take some decisive action or a concern about something beyond my control.

I list the issue and make a note on my mobile about what needs to happen to address this concern if it is something I can act on. I will then write only one step that I can take today to solve the problem. I set up a reminder to come back to that phase later when I have more time to answer it correctly. Only making these notes helps to relieve anxiety.

If it's something that's totally out of my control, I do as outlined above, The DARE Answer. With a "whatever" attitude, I defuse the nervous "what if" feelings, I recognize that I have no control over, and I gently shift my mind back to interacting with what I was doing. I will have to do this many times, but the issue will eventually lose its burden and become less intrusive.

Worry Over Thoughts

You may find yourself going from worries about stuff to worries about thoughts after an extended period of high anxiety. This is where it can transform the imaginative mind on itself.

Intrusive or unsettling thoughts about subject matters are the kind of thoughts I'm referring to here that shock you only because you had that particular thought.

Typical intrusive thoughts frequently revolve around gender or misunderstanding regarding sexual identity, blasphemous thoughts, or behaving violently against loved ones spontaneously.

People suffering from persistent intrusive thoughts say such things as:

"I can't control them, and they're scaring me. At odd times, they keep popping up.'

What if a part of me tries to do this awful thing in which I keep thinking? What if the sign is that I'm losing control?

I feel like I have to suppress these thoughts, or else they will take over. Starting to fear for your well-being or getting frustrated when unwanted thoughts manifest is perfectly natural. Still, you have to remember they are nothing more than the product of elevated stress hormones + mental fatigue.

The very fact that you react to these thoughts with anxiety proves that you're perfectly normal. You don't lose it, nor are you a poor person for worrying about it. You only suffer from the side effects of elevated anxiety.

Thinking occurs ... and that's not how you are.

It's not reality; a thought is just a thought. The fact that you believe something does not make it so, nor does it reflect on the person you are. Don't mistake the substance of your thoughts for the person you are. They do not reflect the real you with these thoughts.

We have about 50,000 thoughts per day, on average. All of them are wacky and bizarre. We've all got them. The only difference is that those thoughts stand out and catch your attention while you feel extremely sensitized. When you respond to them in terror, you feel a jolt of panic, like an electric zap.

You may have an out-of-the-blue idea, for instance, driving the kids to school: "What if I just swerved into the coming car?" Zap!-Zap!

You respond in panic, and you feel in your stomach the jolt of fear. The thought alone is enough to knock the wind out of you right away.

How could I ever have thought of such a thing? I must have gone nuts! Zap, zap! Zap! All this self-doubt and fear leads to more anxious feelings, and in the vicious loop of anxiety, you are back again.

Other common examples of this may be:

What if I had just jumped from the balcony...?

What if I don't even love my wife anymore...?

What if, right now, I did something utterly inappropriate...?

Everyone's initial reaction is to respond to such thoughts in fear and then try to drive them away, but this is the main error we all make.

The more you drive away from your mind, those feelings, the harder they come back. Remember when you played in the pool with an inflatable beach ball as a child?

It just kept springing back up with the same force you used to hold it down each time you tried to bring it down under the water to sit on it, sometimes hitting you on the face. For these intrusive feelings, the same goes.

By driving them away, you really can't hope to get peace from them. The only way to create peace is to allow a beach ball to float next to you.

You have to avoid reacting to the thoughts that terrify you and learn to embrace and allow them with fear. I don't assume that you agree with the thought's substance when I say "accept and allow" an intrusive thought. I mean, you're embracing the concept of what it is, a random thought formed by an anxious mind and nothing more. Let me give you an example of how you can apply these distracting thoughts to The DARE Answer.

Note, unwanted thoughts or fears can not be managed; only your reaction to them can be controlled. Let's say you cut the vegetables for dinner, for instance, and your partner comes into the kitchen and gets something out of the fridge.

An unwelcome thought crosses your mind as they have their back to you: 'What if I lost control and stabbed him/her with this knife in the back? You must have felt the old one punch you in the stomach with a jolt of fear and maybe even scare you enough to put the knife back in your drawer.

The new you, using The DARE Response's theory, do not put down the knife but continues slicing and begins to defuse the nervous "what if."

What if I just stabbed him/her randomly with this knife? Oh well, I'd get locked up then.

I will no longer have to make dinner, at least! You defuse the nervous feeling, instead of being frightened by it, by being flippant or sarcastic about it.

Use whatever answer you believe accomplishes the objective. It's a bit like the way you might react to a little kid walking into the room dressed like a monster trying to scare you.

"Hey, you are so big and frightening!". With a wry smile, you say.

Then allow without any resistance to the intrusive thinking being present. Let it stay as long as it needs to. Recall the example of a beach ball. It will bounce back if you try to force it down, just let it be present and then gently move your mind back to what you have been doing. Some thoughts can have a highly persistent disposition on days when you feel very nervous. As they stick to you, I call it a "high glue factor"! This is where you can enforce The DARE Response's "rush toward" phase. You can get excited and demand more of it instead of just recognizing and embracing the idea, to shake yourself loose from its grasp.

"Oh, it's a strange idea to do something utterly inappropriate again. Today it seems really powerful. All right — so let's have it! I'm going to worry all day about this. Come on, let's see if I can think of things that are even more odd than that.'"

Finally, participate in whatever is at hand. In this situation, while not moving the thought aside, you shift your focus back to making the meal.

You can have to do the above measures many times in a row with really intrusive ideas any time the intrusive thoughts grab hold of you. You normalize them until you eliminate the emotional reaction to unwanted thoughts, and they do not have an emotional pull anymore. If they no longer have a pull, they inevitably fall apart on their own, as they have little to cling to.

Chapter 11

GIVE UP YOUR SAFE ZONE

I want you to push yourself even more now that we are further into the novel and force yourself to bravely step beyond your safe zone. It is where true learning and development occurs.

Every nervous individual has a secure zone in which they feel safe. This safe zone can be familiar places such as their home or their neighborhood, or they can be with a support person who understands and supports them wherever they are. It seems that safe zones make us feel secure that all is manageable. The problem is that they're a self-imposed jail.

It's where the person wants to spend more and more time because comfort is found there. The anxiety issue is that when the safe zone becomes just the four walls of a person's home (agoraphobia), it continues to invade everything.

A myth is the protected zone. There's no such thing as a safe zone against anxiety. As there is nothing life-threatening about a panic attack, sitting at home is no more of a risk than sitting under the stars in Australia's outback. Your mind rushes instantly to tell you, of course, that Australia's outback is a ridiculous place to be because there are no hospitals, no tranquilizers, no doctors, no protection.

Study your past anxiety and panic attack symptoms. After all those attacks during which you were sure that you were going to die, aren't you still here, alive and well?

You may have been taken to the hospital on occasion, where you were medicated to calm you down. But do you truly believe that if it were not for the medications, you would not have survived? You'd have. If in the middle of nowhere the same bout of fear had happened and you were all alone, it would have also gone. Yeah, it is a huge advantage to have medical assistance nearby when it comes to illnesses that require medical treatment, such as asthma, diabetes, and a whole litany of other conditions. But no doctor in the world can say to an anxious person that there are only such safe zones where he or she can travel.

So I want you to really force yourself beyond your safe zone right now. In your head, cross the red line and go for it. I just want you to dig deep and push out like you never did before. Only reading what you need to do is never enough; you have to feel it. True progress and learning happen when we question ourselves when we experience pressure and reach beyond our levels of comfort. We must, as Susan Jeffers wrote, "feel the fear and do it anyway."

Today, are you willing to feel the fear?

I know more than anyone how scary it can feel to step out of your safe zone as within the anxiety bubbles up, but you have what it takes to do this. You're powerful enough, I know. If you weren't, you wouldn't have read too far into the novel.

The difference, of course, is that you now have a specific tool (The DARE Response) as well as my audio form help for you to take with you everywhere you go between now and the last time you tried anything like this.

I will send you an example of how you can do this. As an example, I'll use driving, but this example applies to any situation where you want to reach forward and question your safe zone.

It's important to split this challenge into steps, as I mentioned previously with driving so that you keep pushing yourself a bit further each day. On the first try, that could mean driving to the end of your street and then the next day around the block.

You apply The DARE Answer as you drive and feel the fear, and then once you realize that you are a considerable way beyond your secure zone, pull over and stay there. In that new room, work through the anxiety.

Don't just turn and rush back home. Rushing home gives the signal that you just made it, but you could have gotten into some trouble if you waited any longer. That's not true, and by proving to yourself that you can actually stay outside your safe zone just fine, you need to counteract those fears. Sure, maybe it's awkward, but hold your ground and don't retreat.

Leave on your own terms, not those of fear. Stay in the new position until you do not feel nervous anymore. That way, you plant your success flag firmly on the ground and claim the new territory as yours. You are outside your old safe zone, and you stayed there and worked through it even though you felt nervous. With a much stronger sense of pride in what you have achieved, you can now return home. You have left your safe zone and accomplished your target. That's a win, really.

Solidify the accomplishment once you get home by writing it down in your journal. To make it all the more real, this is very significant. Then write down immediately what your next objective is going to be.

Are you going to drive a few blocks south, perhaps? Will you try driving in traffic, maybe? If you are ready for it or allow yourself a day's rest, you can do it the next day. The main thing is not to leave it for more than a couple of days, or fear will sneak in and take the soil back from you. Don't allow that. Keep going and always push this unseen boundary farther out.

The illusion of a safe zone will suddenly evaporate if you keep this momentum going. No matter where you are, whether out in the wilderness or in a crowded place or even flying over the Atlantic, you will begin to feel genuinely safe and comfortable inside yourself. That liberty comes from pushing and never giving up through any setback. When that happens, it varies from person to person, but you can be confident that you'll get there if you stick to it.

Yes, you're allowed, of course, to have days off. If you feel you are not ready for it, I don't want you to push yourself too hard. When you just don't feel up to it and want to crawl under the covers, there will be days. That's all right; allow for those down days, but then pick yourself up and get out there again once your vitality returns. Build up the emotional momentum once again and be relentless.

Continue to press through!

I know some of you might think that because it's difficult to duplicate (e.g., traveling or public speaking), you can't easily practice your particular fear, but there are ways to place yourself in circumstances that induce a similar fear in which you can practice. For instance, in tall skyscrapers, a man I coached who had a claustrophobic fear of sitting in an airplane would use elevators to practice working through his fear. To practice his delivery, another man who wanted to conquer his fear of talking at work meetings used a weekly Toastmasters club. Be imaginative. There are still opportunities to come up with scenarios under which you know that will give you a similar fear in which you will challenge yourself.

If you want a swift recovery, it is located beyond your safe zone, feeling and working through the anxiety. Being out there in the world, feeling nervous and working through it is so much better than living in an imaginary bubble of safety.

Don't expect to like it when you push beyond your safe zone, even though it's a fun activity, like going to the movies or dining out with friends. Like homework, handle it. It'll just feel weird in the early days as you'll be so focused on the challenge, but you'll gradually start to enjoy doing it as you continue to practice.

Now, take a moment and decide to do so. I just want you to go for it, just as your life depends on it. Is there anything more meaningful that you should strive towards? You fight to take back your liberty.

PANIC ATTACKS!

Chapter 12

GIVE UP BEING SO HARD ON YOURSELF

People who suffer from depression appear to be incredibly harsh on themselves. The more there is fear, the worse it gets. If they suffered from a physical condition such as diabetes, these people would not give themselves such a hard time. Still, they certainly abuse themselves for having a mental health disorder such as anxiety.

I assume the explanation for this is that some of them think it's their fault. There is accompanying guilt of being vulnerable to fear and anxiety because of feeling frail. It can lead to feelings of depression and isolation once this form of negative self-talk creeps in. After each episode of anxiety, Patrick, who has been a great contributor to my coaching program, calls it the "collateral damage" he used to do to himself every day.

You're a very kind guy, I bet. The only issue is that maybe you're not so kind to yourself. Maybe you're your own worst critic. Why would that be? Why are we so much better off treating others than we do ourselves? I'm sure you would be positive and compassionate if your best friend suffered from anxiety and wouldn't dream of regularly doing the kind of things you say to yourself.

As another member of the coaches put it:

For three years, I have had therapy, and it has always been pointed out to me how hard I am on myself. For me, the goodness and compassion I have shown to others are never there.

And where does he come from with this strong self-criticism? In my view, much of it is fueled by a simple lie. It's a lie that you aren't good enough. It's so easy. You believe to like. In some way, you're flawed and not worthy. You risk being rejected or abandoned by others for not being good enough while you believe this lie.

This same lie is believed by much of the human race, and, as a result, many of us suffer from low self-esteem. This is why public speaking is often referred to as the number one fear of people since public speaking opens us to immediate rejection.

This single lie is the source of so much unhappiness and, in severe situations, even self-hatred, you are not good enough. This problem of low self-worth becomes magnified when things go wrong, such as when anxiety manifests.

I'm going to concentrate on the solution in this brief chapter. As you'll have gathered by now, I just suggest easy and efficient therapeutic methods that can be easily enforced.

To overcome low self-esteem, each therapy has its own set of steps and procedures. Today's most common therapy (CBT) will resolve this issue by helping the client recognize and replace unhealthy negative thinking habits with healthier and more effective ones.

While this can be successful, because of the constant effort needed to track and replace these negative thoughts, I think this therapeutic approach also fails to resolve low self-esteem problems. After a week or two, individuals begin to lose patience with the exercise because of the tiring effort involved. The other explanation why many people struggle with this method is that it doesn't go far enough into the problem's heart. It fails to answer the lie hidden deep within the psyche of the individual. Instead of digging it up by the roots, it is more like a gardener only snipping what he can see of a weed.

Finding a very easy strategy that has the power to end this lie by rewiring your level of self-worth is what works even better. This chapter goes beyond the reach of only curing anxiety and touches the field of self-development in transformation. If you feel this is not something you want to look at right now, and then feel free to skip it, but because of the positive impact this exercise can have on the quality of your life, please consider coming back to it at a later time.

I've had a keen interest in personal growth ever since I was a teenager. I've attended countless workshops and seminars worldwide on self-development and read hundreds of books on the subject. I've had the chance to meet many fantastic teachers as well as a couple of charlatans since working in the self-help space supporting people with anxiety for over ten years. The amount of time I spent researching personal development material did not turn me by any stretch of imagination into an enlightened person. But it gave me the ability to quickly distinguish between methods that work and those that don't.

When I say that what follows might be the most effective self-help exercise you'll come across; I'm not exaggerating.

Chapter 13

GIVE UP FEARING IT WILL LAST FOREVER

One of the most prevalent concerns when in the mire of anxiety is that the feeling will last forever. In your life, this prison without walls will become a permanent reality. You project into the future and see only suffering, always having to live with the constraint and avoidance generated by fear of anxiety.

When you're in the throes of such depressing feelings, with this one though, you may soften the emotion:

This will pass, too.

And it is going to.

"Fear is finite; hope is infinite", Shervin Pishevar wrote. You have to preserve your confidence and hope that your condition will improve. Things will get better when you least expect it.

You may not believe it right now, but under all these nervous feelings, the person you dream of, the one willing to go wherever you want, to do whatever you want, is waiting there. Those nervous emotions blow through like hurricanes; however, you feel like this storm will run out of rain. They finally clear, and the bright-blue sky emerges again, no matter how gloomy and chaotic.

It is beautiful to watch the darkness of the sky and clouds just before the break of dawn as if to herald some fantastic event that is going to take place from nowhere. For recovery from anxiety, it's always the same. You get the breakthrough you were hoping for right as you think it's at its worst. Right now, if you can't see clearly, keep fast and wait for the day to break.

Oh, don't give up!

People also ask me if I experience anxiety anymore. It's a good question because you want to get an idea of what full recovery looks like or whether a complete recovery is ever possible if you've been suffering from constant anxiety or panic attacks.

Life is stressful, and anxiety is always going to be part of our lives, but the difference is that I'm not stuck in the anxiety loop, so it no longer grows into a "disorder." Let me digress briefly and tell you about a real storm that helps to clarify this argument that I was recently caught up in.

My wife is Brazilian, and on many occasions, we were lucky to visit and explore her amazing country. On one specific ride, we were in a small wooden canoe on the Amazon River with some other tourists and a 14-year-old boy acting as our guide.

It's natural to have a burst of fear come to mind in conditions like that, where you're surrounded by fish with sharp teeth and nowhere to disembark.

What if I want to get off, really?

What if the canoe happens to something?

And what if...? And what if...? And what if...?

I instantly found how the anxiety had baited me, so I enforced The DARE Answer.

The flash fright subsided within seconds, and I was back to feeling excited and ready. I stepped out of a potential state of fear and connected with the moment. The old me might easily have reached a state of high anxiety or panic, but in a situation like that, armed with The DARE Response, I had a new empowered response. As it turns out, something really happened, but I was in the best frame of mind to respond to it because of the DARE answer.

We were led too far downstream by our young guide and didn't pay attention to how late it was. As it turns out, every day in the afternoon, it rains really hard, and it's not a safe idea to be in a canoe with so many people when it rains. To make it worse, none of us had a life jacket to wear. Heavy rain began to fall as we turned the canoe over to head home.

This was an exceptionally heavy downpour; every drop looked the size of a marble! In front of your face, you could scarcely see your side. A school of hungry piranha fish swam below us. There was a scramble to place cameras in waterproof plastic bags, and my wife turned to our guide and asked if this kind of rain was safe for me to be out.

His little concerned face said it all. Não!- (No!)- It only took about one minute before the canoe contained an inch or two of water, and we would quickly capsize if it kept filling up like that.

The vegetation on either side was too dense for disembarkation, so the only choice was to get home quickly. I never had fear overcoming me through all this; instead, I was able to keep my mind calm in a moment of a true emergency. It was, in the end, a huge empty bottle of coke that had rescued us.

The initiative was taken by a Japanese student and me to cut the Coke bottle in half with a penknife, and then we used both ends to bail out the water as easily as it came in. That afternoon, we bailed the water out like Olympic sportsmen. We managed to prevent the water from rising above our ankles with that team effort and finally made it back to the lodge. When we made it back, our guide was obviously surprised but relieved.

He tried to make his nervous father, who was waiting for us on the jetty, aware of it. The rest of us, happy to be alive and in search of a stiff Caipirinha, disembarked. The reason I am telling you this story is not to brag, but to prove that you motivate yourself to behave better in any situation when you decide to have a new answer to your anxiety. It's also fun often to play MacGyver!

Setbacks And How To Deal With Them

A new "what if" fear creeps in when a person starts making some positive strides in his or her relationship with anxiety.

What happens if the fear returns? What if I get plunged back into fear in my prison cell?

This fear is quite prevalent. Doubting your newfound liberty is understandable.

It's almost guaranteed, honestly, that you're going to have a big setback. I have mentored a few individuals who have not had failures during their recovery to independence. There is an old English proverb that says, "a smooth sea never made a professional sailor." In order to gain your freedom, failures are like final-stage exams you have to get through. After you have had a substantial achievement, failures are especially normal, such as doing something you were previously nervous about, e.g., overcoming a big challenge or after a significant life event such as moving home, changing jobs, etc. You should expect them and accept them, as it's almost a certainty that you will encounter setbacks!

You will drop the anger you feel and pass through them at greater speed if you truly realize that failures are part of the healing process.

The shock it gives you is the most disturbing thing about getting a setback. There you were, making great strides, and then unexpectedly, the anxiety struck you heard from out of the blue.

Not only do you feel like you're back at Square One, but you're now afraid that you're never going to be free of anxiety and that any progress you've made has been an illusion. Dr. Reid Wilson speaks about the meaning of learning to "love the mat." It's an expression of martial arts that means that every now and then, you have to prepare to be thrown to the floor. You don't get irritated by it when you suspect it.

Instead, you actually come to understand that it is just part of the creation and learning process. It makes you more strong. It is important to learn to retrain how you respond to setbacks. The mistaken reaction prolongs the setback.

With much greater ease, the right answer moves you through it. The correct response is The DARE Answer. Start by defusing the "what ifs" that occur anxiously. What if all the progress I have been making was an illusion?

What if this never gets rid of me?

What if, by trying to end it, I've made my anxiety worse? Defuse each of these questions with a firm declaration of dismissal, such as: "Alright, whatever.

I think then I'm only going to feel nervous if that's the way it's going to be today.

Next, allow that to be a setback; don't fight it. Actually, welcome it and see it as part of your continued growth.

Let go of having to go away and embrace uncomfortable anxiety and allow it to be exactly as it is today. Enable this loss to happen to yourself. It's not forever, mind. It's all shifting, and this storm is going to pass.

Finally, stop dwelling on the setback when you're prepared and connect with something to prevent your nervous mind from ruminating on the setback.

Chapter 14

GIVE UP YOUR CRUTCHES

This is a brief chapter, but for you, it contains an important final challenge. To reach full recovery, you need to pass this challenge. You'll have acquired one or more crutches if you've suffered from anxiety for any substantial amount of time. Crutches may be people you rely on or things you use in anxious times to make you feel reassured and safe.

Any common examples of this may be:

- Always have a safe individual with you;

- Never leave home without getting your mobile phone;

- Still in your pocket with a Xanax;

- Carrying around with you a small bottle of alcohol;

- Messaging people any time you feel nervous, or calling them;

- Having carried out the same medical examinations over and over again;

In order to feel secure, crutches are any external thing that you feel you need. As they provide a safety net of sorts, it's understandable how crutches grow. You say to yourself, "Ok, I'll still have X to depend on if things get really rough." If you think about it, having a crutch is a sign that you still don't completely believe that you're secure. Crutches are a sign that the history of anxiety is still fighting you.

Crutches are really useful in the early stages of rehabilitation to get you up and walking towards your target. If you were to break your leg, you'd need crutches to get you moving and moving. You then need to discard the crutches after a certain point in order to stand securely on your own two legs.

Here is how the process of giving up his biggest crutch (his wife) was represented by Ian.

Since entering the program, I believe I've made amazing progress. I'm doing stuff I haven't tried in years. Panic and anxiety do not have the same effect on me that they used to have. Currently, I haven't had an actual full-on panic attack in a couple of months now. There's still plenty of ground to cover, and I don't feel like I'm out of the woods yet, but I feel most optimistic about the road I'm on now. I read a post about "crutches" this afternoon in the "members" area. This got me thinking, and I had a nice chat with my wife then. I demonstrated to her that I am now being held back by the encouragement she offers me. I thanked her for being there for me at all times, for doing the stuff I feel I can't do, for being my business when I have to drive past my comfort zone.

I clarified to her that I know she's doing all these things because she thinks she's helping me, and I thought so, but from now on, no matter what, she's never going to allow me to use her again as a "crutch."

I love my wife with all my heart, and I have no idea how without her, I would have been able to get through the last six years, but now it's time to remove my crutch and begin this journey alone.

This conversation with her, of course, made me nervous. It brought me a bunch of what-ifs. ... What if I'm not ready, or if I have a bad day, or if I'm not as far down the path to recovery as I think I am, and I still need her...?

I'm expecting my anxiety levels to increase again in the next few weeks and maybe even a return of panic attacks, but for me, this is now the next step I need to take, and it's too late even if I change my mind. I had a talk with her and asked her, "No matter what I say, this is the way to support me now."

It was dramatic and took a lot of bravery to do what Ian did. Part of him recognized the plateau of his rehabilitation, and he had to take this plunge and abandon his crutch in order to get to the next level.

I'm not saying that you ought to discard your crutches with the same taste as Ian did, but at least try to start the process in incremental stages and wean yourself off your crutches.

For instance, you could decide today to go alone for a drive instead of taking your safe person with you. Maybe when you go out for a walk, you should leave your phone or Xanax at home. Or maybe you might plan to go shopping on your own locally.

Whatever it is that you do with your crutch at all times, start planning ways to practice without it. Try to do one little thing without a crutch every day. It doesn't have to be a huge thing; it's important to keep moving it out so that you build up your confidence like a muscle.

I know that in the initial stages, this can be very difficult to do, especially if you've relied on your crutch for many years, but now you have to dig deep and find courage. For this challenge, you are well prepared because you now have The DARE Answer to replace your crutch. Anytime you feel nervous, it will teach you to depend entirely on yourself.

With a crutch still in place, it is, of course, possible to have a decent degree of recovery, but you may never feel like you've made it all the way. There will be this niggle of anxiety that will keep plaguing you, telling you that as you still rely on your crutch to feel protected, you are still vulnerable. In the long run, the niggle can weaken your confidence, and that's why it's so important to take on this final challenge.

Commit yourself to do so now. To discard your crutches, build a workable plan so that you can make a complete recovery.

Walk forward through each new day bravely.

Anti-procrastination techniques:

Break large tasks into smaller ones

It can encourage you to take action by splitting large tasks into smaller sub-tasks, making large tasks feel less daunting, and allowing you to experience a continuous stream of rewarding progress. In addition, doing this often helps you from an organizational point of view by helping you identify exactly what you need to do to accomplish your goals and by allowing you to make plans that provide a high degree of detail.

For instance, you can break down the big task of writing the paper into an ordered list of subtasks that you need to perform if your goal is to write a paper for a class. Subtasks such as "decide on a subject" can be included in this list, followed by "collect a list of relevant sources," "write the introduction," etc.

There are a few things you should keep in mind when using this technique:

You can break tasks apart as much as you want. A good rule of thumb is to build subtasks that require no longer than a single session to complete, ensuring that before you need to take a break, you can finish them.

If it helps, start with a small first step. In order to make it easier for you to get over the initial hurdle of actually getting started, some people feel that it helps to start with a small first step.

You don't have to outline the entire project from the start. If you deal with a big project, you don't have to begin by detailing all of its next steps, and it may even be counterproductive to do so. Instead, beginning by finding out only the next few steps you need to tackle, and then adding new ones later, after you've made enough progress, is always preferable.

Prioritize Tasks

You will find out which tasks you need to work on and when you need to work on them by prioritizing your tasks. This will ensure that by spending time on insignificant tasks while neglecting serious ones; you do not end up procrastinating, which will also help you avoid circumstances where you feel stressed because you are not sure where to start or what tasks you should be working on.

The following are two common methods for prioritizing your tasks:

The Ivy Lee method:

At the end of each day, this approach includes preparing a to-do list and writing down a list of six things that you want to finish tomorrow, ranked in order of priority.

The Eisenhower Matrix:

This strategy includes categorizing each role you have based on whether it is crucial or unimportant and on whether it is urgent or not urgent and then prioritizing your duties based on these parameters.

Overall, to prioritize your activities, there are several strategies you may use. Don't waste time over-optimizing or getting stuck, finding out which one to use your prioritization method; just pick one to start with and then try different methods before you find out which one works best for you. Just go with the Ivy Lee form, which is explained above, if you are unsure about this.

Use time-management techniques

To make it easier for yourself to get started on your job and to keep focused once you have started, you can use different time-management strategies.

For instance, to coordinate your workflow, you can use the **Pomodoro Technique**, which is a time-management technique where you use a timer. Before beginning to work again, the Pomodoro Method involves focusing on the tasks for a fixed period of time (e.g., 25 minutes) and then taking a brief break (e.g., 5 minutes). In addition, as part of Pomodoro, you can take a longer break (e.g., 30 minutes) after you complete a certain number of work cycles (e.g., four cycles) before returning to work.

To suit your personal tastes, you can change this technique and similar ones. For instance, you might opt to use a different metric, such as the number of words you have written or the number of pages you have read, instead of using a fixed period of time to limit each work cycle while using the Pomodoro Technique.

There is no one approach that works well for everyone, so before you find the one that works for you, you can try out different methods. If you're not sure which one to begin with, just go with the Pomodoro Technique and change it as you go along to suit your needs.

Use a to-do list

For many factors, using a to-do list is incredibly helpful when it comes to helping you stop procrastinating:

- It lets you break down your goals into tasks that are actionable;

- It lets you coordinate, prioritize, and optimally plan your assignments;

- It allows you to concentrate only on particular tasks that you need to think about at the moment;

- It allows you to write and stick with deadlines;

- It lets you track your progress and find out what works and what doesn't work for you.

Furthermore, you can also get extra incentive to focus on your projects by using a to-do list because it makes you want to be able to mark certain tasks off your list and because you get additional gratification from being able to do so.

You can either use the pen-and-paper process or one of the many applications on the market when it comes to making your to-do list. Until you find the one that works best for you, try different options, but as always, make sure not to get stuck over-optimizing things, and simply choose one choice, to begin with at first. You can still reassess the situation if necessary, and change your solution as you move along.

PANIC ATTACKS!

Chapter 15

REWARD YOURSELF FOR YOUR ACCOMPLISHMENTS

People also procrastinate because important long-term activities that are rewarding for them are less desirable than less advantageous short-term habits that feel more rewarding. As such, by associating incentives that are fun in the short-term with acts that are beneficial for you in the long-term, you will reduce the risk that you will procrastinate.

For example, for every chapter you read in preparation for a test, you might decide to take a quick break and watch some TV, or you could eat a small piece of chocolate as a reward for every task you complete while working on a project.

Similarly, by doing easy things like writing down any task you perform during the day and then looking through them at night to see how much you have managed to get accomplished, you can also make your successes more fulfilling.

Notice that you can reward yourself either for beginning, completing, or working on a task in general. Rewards should be provided for activities that are sufficiently meaningful to allow you to make progress but are still sufficiently accessible to encourage you in the short term.

Eliminate distractions

Removing distractions from your environment means that you are more able to concentrate on your job and stop procrastinating.

For instance, if every time you get a message, your phone emits a loud sound, you will constantly be distracted as you work, which will make it difficult for you to concentrate. As such, you would want to place your phone in silent mode in such situations when you are working or use a dedicated app to disable alerts, which will help you focus on your job.

You should bear in mind the detrimental effect that even seemingly minor distractions can have on you while doing this.

The study, for example, indicates that even though you're not consciously using your phone, it's a big distraction to simply have it on your desk. In addition, while it can minimize the degree to which it acts as a diversion by putting your phone inside your pocket, having the phone, there still consumes more of your mental energy than having it in a separate room, where it is completely out of control.

Another example of this problem is the fact that multitasking is related to decreased levels of self-control by doing items such as watching TV or browsing social media while participating in cognitive tasks such as learning, which in turn will make you more likely to procrastinate.

Research indicates that reciprocal causality is possibly involved in the relationship between this form of multitasking and low levels of self-control. This suggests that people with lower levels of self-control are more likely to multitask in this way when they are working, but this multitasking is also likely to reduce the ability of people to control themselves while they are working.

Make it harder for yourself to procrastinate

The harder you make it for yourself to indulge in procrastinatory practices, the more you will be able to stop procrastinating yourself.

For instance, blocking the sites that you usually look at when procrastinating will make it harder for you to procrastinate if you need to write a paper on your laptop, and you prefer to procrastinate by browsing social media. This would dramatically increase the chances that you will get to work, simply because you don't have much else to do.

Make it easier to get started on tasks.

The simpler it is for you to get started on tasks you need to do, the more likely you are to complete them in a timely manner.

For instance, if you need to work on that kind of document, then you can leave it open on your computer before you go to sleep so that when you turn on your computer in the morning, it will be the first thing you will see, which will increase the chance that you will work on it.

Make unpleasant tasks more enjoyable.

The more stressful a particular job is, the more likely you are to procrastinate on it in general. As such, you decrease the chance that you will procrastinate on them by making unpleasant tasks more appealing.

There are several ways that you can find assignments more desirable. For instance, you can put on music that you like if you need to clean the house and try to time yourself to see how much you can get done in a 10-minute work sprint to make this otherwise boring job more enjoyable.

Set time constraints for decision-making

If you tend to procrastinate because you are struggling to make decisions promptly, by setting arbitrary time limits for yourself.

For instance, you can set a timer with 1 minute on it if you need to decide which design scheme to use in a presentation, and decide that once the timer runs out, you have to go with one of the options available, even if you're not perfectly sure it's the right one.

This approach is particularly helpful in circumstances where you do not have any new knowledge to take into account or in situations where the choice you need to make is not that important in the first place, such as when none of the choices available is substantially better than the others, which means that it doesn't matter which one you choose.

Use countdowns

The countdown is a process where you pick a number and then count down until you hit zero from that number, at which point you have to take some action.

You can decide, for instance, to have a five-second rule, where you count down from five, and you have to get started on your job once you finish the countdown, no matter what.

By training yourself to abide by them, you can make countdowns more effective. In essence, this means that before engaging in relatively straightforward and simple activities that you do regularly, you should use countdowns, which would make you more likely to follow through on them until it comes to more complicated and aversive tasks.

Start with your best or worst tasks.

Some people find it helpful to start their day by coping with the job they fear most, so they can get it out of the way immediately and go through the rest of the day feeling that they've already taken care of it. This method is referred to as eating the frog or eating the elephant beetle, where the 'frog' means that you have to take care of the unpleasant task.

Alternatively, to help themselves get started and enter the right attitude they need for work, some individuals find it more advantageous to begin with, their simplest tasks first.

Both choices are perfectly appropriate, so you can try them both to find out which one works for you while keeping in mind that in various situations, each of them could work better.

Immediately complete small tasks

One way to stop procrastinating on small tasks is to have them completed whenever you can do so, as soon as you find out that you need to do them. This has the added advantage of stopping the piling up of these tiny tasks until they become daunting, which is also much more productive than wasting time preparing these tasks later.

This theory is often referred to as the 2-minute rule, to show how short a job should be for you to quickly want to take care of it. It's up to you, though, to determine how small a job needs to be for you to enforce this law, and the important thing is not just how long it takes but if you're going to benefit from taking care of it as soon as you find out you need to do it.

Notice that this definition reflects one of two potential variations of the 2-minute rule; the other, covered in the previous entry ('start with a small step'), implies that by committing to just spending a small amount of time on them, you can get yourself started on tasks.

Switch between tasks

Try switching to a new task for a while before returning to the original tasks you were procrastinating if you find yourself procrastinating on something because you feel stuck.

Doing this is useful even though you would prefer to work on the original task preferably, as it is easier to do something less important than doing nothing at all, and because switching between tasks at your discretion will allow you to become "unstuck" when it is time to return to the original task.

Take a break

Taking a short break will sometimes help you clear your head, mentally recharge and find the inspiration you need to get started with your job.

If you've just finished writing a report, for example, and are now procrastinating on your computer instead of beginning your next task, getting up from the computer and taking a quick break could help you reset your mind and turn it back to working mode.

Try to consciously use them to help yourself recharge, and approach them like you would any other job, to make the most of your breaks. For instance, it would be better to take five minutes to get up from the computer and stretch your legs before returning to work instead of taking a break that consists of searching social media before you feel ready to work again.

Figure out what you're afraid of

People also procrastinate because they fear something, whether doing poorly on a job or receiving negative reviews from others. You can better cope with your anxiety by recognizing why you're nervous about a mission, which can help you get started on your job.

For instance, if you know you're postponing starting a new hobby because you're afraid you're going to embarrass yourself, you can speak to people in the group to overcome this fear, which will help you get started.

What Is Mindfulness Meditation?

Meditation on Mindfulness is a method of relaxation that takes the attention back to the present. The meditator allows thoughts to emerge during mindfulness practice without attempting to interrupt or evaluate them. Unpleasant thoughts related to fear, judgment, blame, and worry can arise, for instance. Mindfulness is the act of remembering and allowing these thoughts to pass.

Meditation on Mindfulness is based on the premise that most people drive their present thoughts and emotions away or ignore them. Some assume that those thoughts would automatically go away if they ignore negative thoughts. Yet mindfulness also makes it possible for you to differentiate from negative thinking by facing thoughts without reaction.

You will create a new approach to fear and anxiety by letting uncomfortable thoughts pass without responding. Over time, and with practice, mindfulness meditation will help build inner harmony, clarity, and peace.

Positive thinking

The first GAD study investigating the effects of manipulating imagery and verbal processing in the longer-term reduction of worry and anxiety is recorded here. The key finding was that, with no substantial variations between conditions, all three groups saw significant reductions in negative intrusions and registered worry and anxiety. The control situation in which participants exercised positive imagery chosen to be unrelated to worry material was surprisingly not substantially different from the circumstances in which alternative positive outcomes of worry subjects were practiced, whether in verbal or imagery form. Thus, it seems that the crucial mechanism underlying the changes observed was to replace any alternative constructive ideation with the normal flow of verbal concern. This suggests that, even if the negative and verbal form of concern leads to its persistence, in order to produce change, there is no need to alter this material directly.

Consistent with this interpretation, while the negative level of intrusions was greatly decreased, they were still classified as moderately or extremely negative when intrusions recurred. In other words, it decreased the frequency of worry-related thoughts but not their negativity by practicing some constructive ideation. In addition, decreased follow-up anxiety was predicted by less negative intrusions during breathing concentration and greater capacity in session 2 to produce positive thoughts and disengage from worry. Along with these post-hoc results, the lack of overall discrepancies between groups again indicates that the changes were attributable to increased willingness to disengage from it and concentrate instead on more constructive material rather than reducing negativity of concern. These results converge on the idea that regular practice will counter the intrusive and distressing properties of concern in replacing worry with optimistic ideation.

One challenge to this conclusion is that the modifications may have happened without any interference in the absence of non-intervention regulation. We also concluded that considering that the effect sizes were high and much larger than would be anticipated in the absence of any medication, this is impossible. Nevertheless, since we did not provide a non-positive condition, we can not infer from the present results that it is appropriate to substitute concern with positive ideation. Instead of the normal quasi-verbal form, also directions to visualize negative outcomes minimize later intrusive thoughts (Hirsch et al., 2015; Stokes and Hirsch, 2010), possibly because the more realistic content of images contributes to findings being perceived as more manageable. However, the additional impact of decreasing the perceived cost of worry results and increasing the perceived capacity to cope was only conditioned involving substituting constructive material (Hirsch et al., 2015).

We can make no claims for clinical efficacy, considering that the present findings were not compared with existing therapies, nor would we suggest that the methods used here can be used as stand-alone interventions. In this research, the GAD volunteers were not receiving care, so the efficacy of these strategies in a clinical population has yet to be known. However, the participants registered significant changes in the worry measures (e.g., in-group effect sizes of approximately two on the PSWQ), and these results were sustained one month later. One clinical implication that needs further review is that, as is the purpose of thought challenging in Cognitive Behavior Therapy, it might not be appropriate to explicitly alter worry-related thought material. In replacing them with some constructive (or other) alternative, future studies may usefully compare the efficacy of challenging negative thoughts versus practice. The latter approach will minimize negative intrusive thoughts and avoid the consequent creation of episodes of concern by increasing the availability of competing thoughts. At the very least, current research findings suggest the need to examine if the alteration of negative material or the enhancement of access to constructive alternatives is similarly or differentially successful in preventing uncontrollable GAD worries.

Supercharge your recovery

Together, we come close to the end of our journey. The DARE Answer, I've introduced you to what I think is the most effective instrument that you can equip to end your anxiety. All you need to break free from anxiety and get you back to living your life to the fullest is that tool alone.

But we're still not at the end of the trip. ... I want to finish by providing you with some more tips and perspectives. Not only can this advice help you speed up the recovery process, but after your recovery, it's also a perfect way to keep anxiety at bay. Anytime I go through a stressful phase, I use the tips below to keep my own anxiety in check.

Some people write entire books on what I'm sharing below, but I've distilled the data down to just the important information you need. Please try as many of the following tips as possible to apply them. They will really supercharge your recovery and ensure a lasting result.

Chapter 16

HEAL WITH YOUR HEART

An old English proverb says, *"Fear knocked at the door; love replied, and there was no one."*

I want to dig further into it and share an experience with you that can really help spur your recovery since you are more familiar with The DARE Answer now.

I've talked about the importance of getting your anxious mind out of the way to really break the anxiety loop, but when you take your anxious mind out of the way, what is actually driving the healing? You'll find stuff like approval, allowance, sympathy, playfulness, and kindness if you look at the core qualities of The DARE Answer. These are the real characteristics that heal anxiety, and they are actually characteristics of the heart.

In the end, it's your heart that cures fear, not your brain. It's a caring heart's light and comfort that lifts the thick fog of anxiety. To a degree, the mind can handle and control fear, but it doesn't have the healing ability to cure it. That power emanates from the heart. It's your heart that enables peace of mind to be restored when your restless mind is taken out of the way.

There is intelligence in your heart, and from your heart comes the voice of a wiser, more grounded human. This voice needs to calm your nervous mind. It's your true and genuine self's voice. It is just about creating a place for this wiser, more caring voice to come to the fore and soothe your anxious mind by practicing allowance and acceptance.

Your heart sees a greater vision that allows you, in a different way, to see your suffering. In this struggle, your heart recognizes the intent and essence and gives you the strength to communicate with life again.

When you're really nervous, the prison without walls ends up stuck in your head all the time. Your heart is capable of throwing open the prison door and setting you free. Via compassionate acceptance, the way it does so is 'It's all right,' says your heart to your nervous mind. "I have this one. I embrace this nervous feeling, and I allow it. You no longer have to hang on so tightly. This gentle, caring embrace of anxiety reassures the anxious mind that, in reality, things are okay. Your mind feels less pressure to try to keep things under control.

Many individuals are not aware that the heart was reclassified as a hormonal gland in 1983. The heart generates substantial hormones, some of which are responsible for reducing the reaction to stress. Atrial natriuretic factor (ANF) is one of those hormones, and its role is to decrease the release of stress hormones in your body.

Also, a strong stress-relieving hormone produced by the heart is another hormone called oxytocin, generally referred to as the "love" hormone. Oxytocin levels go up when we embrace or kiss a loved one. The release of the hormone, which activates your relaxation response, is triggered by moments of empathy and compassion.

You activate the secretion of these stress-reducing hormones by adopting an attitude of compassionate acceptance towards your anxiety. So, when I speak of the healing powers of the heart, both metaphorically and physically, I mean it.

Love Heals Fear

It is a message passed down across the ages. Sadly, for practical application to a situation such as an anxiety disorder, the idea is too abstract. A practical application of that wisdom is the DARE Answer. With heartfelt concern at its center, it's a therapeutic approach.

As a leading research center on the neuroscientific impact of compassion and mindfulness, the Max Planck Institute for Human Cognitive and Brain Sciences has conducted a major study called the ReSource Project in Germany. The results of this project demonstrated what thousands of other studies have shown, which is that participants have major stress-reducing effects on meditation and mindfulness. What was most noteworthy in their results, however, was that their stress levels fell significantly lower when participants were focused on compassion-based activities compared to using only mindfulness alone. What their research has shown is that feelings of compassion can significantly decrease the stress levels of an individual.

We need to practice having more compassion for ourselves in order to get the full stress-reducing effects of compassion. We all seem to beat ourselves way too often to have an anxiety problem, as I discussed previously. You begin a profound change in the way you feel about yourself and your anxiety when you start to follow an approach like The DARE Answer. The key to minimizing stress and enhancing your own self-image and self-worth is to cultivate a respectful acceptance of who you are and what you're experiencing.

Only now in therapeutic practice is mainstream psychology beginning to understand the transformative potential of working with compassion. We see a real rise in interest in therapies such as cognitive therapy focused on mindfulness (MBCT) and acceptance and commitment therapy (ACT), which are essentially heart-centered therapies. As stated earlier, as they outperform older therapeutic methods, I expect these heart-centered therapeutic approaches will grow in popularity over the coming years.

The true healer is your spirit. You're not only working to minimize your anxiety in the best way possible when you practice The DARE Answer, but you're also working to boost your sense of self-worth, which will supercharge your recovery!

Water

Water is the next instrument that I want you to use to supercharge your recovery. Water is a great thirst quencher, but most importantly, here, it is a great anxiety quencher. There is no easier way than drinking fresh water to decrease general anxiety significantly.

The efficient flow of water through our system is related to almost every function of the body. Water carries the body's vital organs with hormones, chemical messengers, and nutrients. Our bodies then begin to respond with a range of signals if we don't keep our bodies well hydrated, some of which are signs of anxiety. Studies have shown that being dehydrated by just half a liter (the equivalent of two cups) will raise your levels of cortisol, making you feel more nervous and on edge.

Your stress response is firing more than normal when you suffer from regular panic attacks, and this causes an accumulation of toxins in your bloodstream that need to be flushed out. This is why keeping yourself well hydrated all the time is so critical.

Drinking eight glasses of freshwater every day is the secret to rebalancing a fluid deficit. You must spread this consumption over the day, however, and not drink all of it in one go. Otherwise, there will be no chance for your body to absorb it, and the excess will only flow through your body. For optimum absorption, drink your water during the day. However, I would warn against drinking too much before bed, just because if you need to use the bathroom in the middle of the night, it could disturb your sleep.

By having water put in strategic areas, the best way to ensure you get enough is to make things convenient for yourself. That might mean you have fresh bottled water in your car, at your desk, or anywhere you know you're spending time. You'll drink it if you put it in visible places. It easily goes out of mind if it is out of sight. You have to make it easy for yourself for any new habit you choose to develop, or else you'll lose it after a few days.

When you know that dehydration is a contributing factor to anxiety and nervousness, you start paying even more attention to how much you drink on a regular basis. Personally, I have discovered that not only does a daily water intake eliminate any slight feelings of anxiety, but it is also extremely useful for building resilience and preventing exhaustion. It is a very simple step to integrate into your everyday routine to increase the amount of freshwater you drink to eight glasses a day, and it can have such an enormous effect on your recovery from anxiety.

CONCLUSION

The whole purpose of this book and The DARE Answer is for you to win back your freedom, without the cloud of fear hanging over you, to get you to live life again. I know that is what you most wish for: to live without having to think about any situation in advance—being willing to go to places without being scared of what could happen before you get there. To spend time without the relentless interruption of nervous thoughts with friends or relatives.

Movement is life. The DARE answer is the way to bring you back to life once more. It is no accident that The DARE Response's last step is "Engage." The step completes the loop and brings you back to the life robbed from you by anxiety. You can see how, in contrast to fear, this movement to live acts. You are taken out of life by fear. The DARE Answer puts you in it right again.

You improve the healing process and heal your anxiety every time you exercise The DARE Answer. That's why I say that even if your anxiety doesn't drop right away, you should never fail to apply The DARE Answer. It is something to celebrate, just the very act of introducing it as it really gets you going in the right direction. Don't put yourself or the process in question. Only trust that it's working, and you'll start to feel a whole lot better within a short period of time. You've got to keep doing this courageous job. Know, the cure is you. It can't be done for you by someone else.

Do you remember that I dared you to imagine what your life would look like at the beginning of the book without anxiety being a problem anymore? Ok, you have the resources now to fully accomplish that. I hope that you can start feeling a lot more optimistic about your future. I hope that the dreams that you may have put on hold are once again beginning to come alive and excite you.

You easily begin to feel more relaxed in your own skin again when you commit to and consistently practice The DARE

Answer. You feel more involved in life and less concerned about circumstances that have always bothered you. Deep down, you eventually start to believe that you can handle it bravely, no matter what happens.

Note, the lack of stimuli is not recuperation. Regardless of what sensations are there, it is about enjoying life and not letting those sensations get in the way of what you want to do. Those feelings gradually slip away all by themselves over time because you no longer pay them any attention.

The only way out is to transfer. There will be setbacks along the way, of course, but they will not discourage you as long as you realize that these setbacks are a vital part of the healing process.

Nobody feels like they're making progress quickly enough in the beginning, but believe me: if you do the job, you're recovering at the right pace for you. You will finally set yourself free by complete acceptance and non-resistance to your nervous sensations.

Soon, one of these nights, you're going to wake up and feel like a layer of fear is falling out of your life. And, a couple of weeks later, another layer is going to come off, and then another layer, and then another layer. You will soon be back to your old self, but you're not exactly the same old self. It's a different, more trusting one that comes about through the mastery of your anxiety.

Your most valuable resource is time. Do not spend any of it on fear anymore. Life awaits you, and you go out and join it! Yeah, I dare you. Too long, you've been gone. About Barry McDonagh

SPREAD THE WORD

To further spread the word that there is a better way to handle anxiety, I need an army of people. Your message could help reach someone who, right now, is suffering in silence. We should shine a light together to let people know that a solution to this issue really exists. Together, we should shift the 'anxiety management' current culture to' anxiety cure. ' Also, if you could leave an honest review on Amazon, I would love it. It can be as short as you want, or as long. For you and your experience with this novel, write whatever is real. Your analysis will talk in the same way that you do to individuals who experience anxiety. Your links will help to improve the lives of many more people who have never found this book before.

COACHING

Often individuals need live assistance to really help them move faster to a complete recovery. Join my coaching program, which runs every month, if you want to. The coaching program is the perfect way to get practical advice and help from professionals who know exactly what you're trying to do.

With greater ease, the insight and assistance you get will really help you accomplish your goals.

Thanks for listening/reading

PANIC ATTACKS!

*If you are interested in Self Help Niche,
here's a small gift for you:
a sneak peek of my new book,*

OVERTHINKING

HOW TO BUILD MENTAL STRENGTH
TO DECLUTTER AND UNFUCK YOURSELF

Eliminate Anxiety and Worrying
In order to Rewire Your Brain
Discovering Fast Your Creativity

DESCRIPTION

Things happen in their own way. Things that we have in control, we try our best to do it in the best way possible. Most of the time we think of the unthinkable future. What might happen, what might the possible outcome be, what might happen if this happens this way or that way, and vice versa. This overthinking is a torture that rots your mind and locks it with a constant array of confused thoughts that feels like hell.

Now ask yourself:

Are you a person who overthinks too much and scared of the outcome?

Are you shackled with your destructive thoughts that just won't go away from your brain?

Then this book is for you that will assist you to stop overthinking and will let you know about the pros and cons of overthinking. Overthinking creates a hindrance in your life and it won't let your live a normal life. Why is that so? These thoughts clutter in your mind and you start suffering from inferiority complex and etc. Trauma and unexpected events happened in someone's past can cause overthinking and they have this constant fear of failing or the outcome of anything. As a result, they get anxiety attacks, depression, and even suicidal thoughts.

This book here can give you step by step guidelines to unfuck your mind and to rediscover yourself and your brain. Eliminating anxiety and mental stress and to reduce the habit of overthinking can lead you to live a life with creativity and more productivity. With this book called "Overthinking", you will have detailed pieces of information on how to get rid of overthinking and anxiety.

Let's take a look at what this book has to offer us:

- ✓ **A brief definition of Overthinking;**

- ✓ **How relationships and past trauma can cause overthinking and how to get rid of it;**

- ✓ **How social media can be overwhelming;**

- ✓ **How to lower expectations and having the mentality to accept everything;**

- ✓ **How to get the peak performance out of yourself.**

Have an amazing life with healthy mind free from destructive thoughts with the help of this book. If you follow the steps and start following it, you will be a person with a more optimistic view who will never be afraid to fail and start from scratches again.

Chapter 1

WHAT IS OVERTHINKING?

Thinking is something we should take them as a blessed ability of humans. We can think before any action or decision, which makes us go easier with life, right?

But what's the factor overthinking?

Why is almost 80% of the population under this?

Why does it sound like an illness?

The questions are innumerable.

Overthinking causes anxiety, stress, fear, dread, etc....

It occurs due to thinking too much without reason, which leads to nothing except own filth. It's common as everyone ends up blaming themselves and regretting it.

Causes of overthinking:

- We often care about people that what they would think if something happened;

- Due to a lack of confidence;

- We assume every problem is centered on us, and instead of solving it, we keep drowning into it by overthinking;

- Imagining useless situations that won't even happen;

- It comes with anxiety that we are often left feeling physically and emotionally unwell;

- Worrying incessantly about who we are and measuring up to the world, which is common in social and performance anxiety;

Thinking — overthinking — a tumbling chain of worries, vague thoughts, and particular thoughts are subject to anxiety disorders that your instinct should address.

Harm of overthinking

The basic and most dangerous thing that can result from overthinking is that we start believing what we are overthinking.

How to not overthink?

Before overthinking starts affecting you better, you start defending it from the beginning.

But how? Mostly, people assume it's a brain factor which can't be fixed.

How Can You Stop Overthinking

- To divert your attention, have something with you or around you. Instead of arguing or obsessing over your thoughts, gently shift your attention to something else;

- Meditating: Guru of all healing, whenever you think your mind is way too loud and garaging. Sitting in silence and admiring calmness can surely give you a way to find peace;

- Physical activity: playing a sport or dancing can release your anxiety through sweat. And you'll be refreshed relieved;

- Try reading a book that enhances self-help and self-growth. I would recommend the book 'Who will cry when you die' by Robin Sharma, which can set you a different vision for life, giving chapters with examples for nurturing minds.

Overthinking works as a barrier as it comforts the unreal situations in your mind and boosts negativity to capture your good path.

Overthinking doesn't just contemplate lives. They conjure up images too. Either way, the tendency to overthink everything holds back from doing something productive and becoming a barrier.

99% of your problems will be solved if you stop overthinking things. So take a deep breath and calm down! Life is about living moments, not overthinking moments.

The habit of overthinking about small things in life is really easy to slip into. Therefore, when you stop and think about something, ask yourself basic questions. It was found that extending the outlook by using these basic questions would easily snap you out of overthinking through an analysis.

Try setting short time-limits for options. So learn by setting deadlines in your everyday life to make choices better and leap into action—no matter whether it's a little decision or a bigger one.

Be a man in motion. If you know how to start taking steps regularly, then by overthinking, you can procrastinate less. One factor that will encourage you to be a person in action is setting deadlines.

Start to understand the one significant point is that you can't control anything. It can be a way to learn to control something by thinking a thing over 50 times so that you cannot make an error, losing or feeling like a fool. All those things are part of living a life where the comfort zone extends.

In a case where you feel you can't think clearly, say pause. Perhaps you start buzzing around in your head when you are starving or lying in bed and are about to go to sleep, and then bad feelings start buzzing about.

Do not get stuck in unclear fears. Another pit you have fallen into several times that spurred overthinking is that you have gotten confused in abstract worries about your life circumstances. And now, the imagination going wild has produced tragic scenarios on what could happen if anything is done. What's the worst thing that could happen? It would help if you learned to ask yourself this question.

Spend much of the time at the moment. In daily life, rather than in the past or a potential future, be in the current moment. Slow down the way you do whatever you do at the moment. Step slower, chat slower, or, for example, ride your bike more slowly. Through doing so, you become more aware of how you use your body right now and what's going on everywhere around you.

Try to spend most of your time with people who do not think more. Your social environment plays a big part. Find ways to spend most of your time and attention with the people and sources that positively affect your thinking.

... What are you waiting for?

Grab a copy today and successfully get improved by yourself on getting rid of **"OVERTHINKING"** and have a healthier mental health.

ABOUT THE AUTHOR STEVE ROBERT CONVEY

Steve Convey was born in New York in 1961.

He attended New York University where he earned a degree in Psychology. In addition to his activity as a university professor and to carry out his profession as a psychoanalyst.

He is also a member of the International Psychoanalytical Association and is on the Board of Directors of the World Association of Infant Mental Health. His studies have often focused on the analysis of relationships between parents and children during childhood. He also explored issues such as the problems of adolescence, the work of the parent, the roles of the family in modern society.

Mr. Convey is stable and caring, but can also be very creative and a bit untidy. Hockey, glamping, and traveling are his favorite things to do. He is an American Christian who defines himself as bisexual.

Steve Convey grew up in a middle-class neighborhood. He was raised in a happy family home with two loving parents.

Steve's best friend is a personal trainer called Mica Wright. They get on well most of the time and they also enjoy walking together.

He is currently married to Evangeline: she is 10 years older than him and works as a Business CEO. They have together 5 five children: Sofia aged 6, Harris aged 12, Ali aged 18, Seth aged 20, and Renee aged 23.

PANIC ATTACKS!